HEALTHY SOY

Cooking with soybeans for health and vitality

HEALTHY SOY

Cooking with soybeans for health and vitality

BRIGID TRELOAR
NUTRITIONIST: KAREN INGE

PERIPLUS

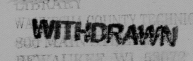

Contents

Introduction

Soybeans have been an important part of Asian diets for centuries. They are often referred to as the "meat of the fields" or "meat without a bone" because they provide more protein than any of the other legumes. Besides being eaten whole—fresh or dried—soybeans are fermented to make miso, tempeh and soy sauce, all of which are used to enhance and add depth to the flavor of both sweet and savory dishes. They are also soaked, mashed and heated to make soy milk and bean curd sheets (yuba), curdled to make tofu (bean curd), and processed to make oil, flour and noodles. Soy foods, in their many different and highly nutritious forms, are remarkably versatile, adapting well to other ingredients and flavors.

It is believed that the soybean, or soya bean, originated in temperate and tropical Africa and Asia. It has been grown for food by the Chinese for thousands of years. It was introduced into Japan from Korea before 200 B.C., but did not appear in Europe until the seventeenth century and the United States until the nineteenth. Often called the "cow of China," it has been the versatile source of many of the high-protein, low-fat products like tofu that the Chinese have used instead of the Western world's dairy equivalents. Today, the range of soy products available in the Western world is ever increasing and includes cheese, yogurt, butter, snacks, desserts, ice cream, pasta and chocolate.

Soybeans are one of the world's richest natural foods: they are high in easily assimilated plant protein, low in fat, contain no cholesterol, and are a good source of soluble fiber. They also provide a rich supply of vitamins and minerals. Some soy foods, such as miso, aid digestion and the absorption of nutrients. And despite all these health benefits, soy foods are relatively inexpensive.

Unfortunately, despite the soybean's many benefits, it is considered by many to be boring, bland and flavorless. But with only a little culinary flair, these nutritional gems can be easily incorporated into the everyday diet to produce enjoyable food with delicious flavors. The culinary potential of soy is endless, limited only by the imagination.

The Health Benefits of Soy

The soybean is a nutritionally unique legume that is becoming more popular in the Western world as its many health and nutritional benefits are recognized. Soy foods have been popular for centuries in Asia, where they form the staple of traditional diets. Much of the research on the health benefits of soy has stemmed from the fact that many Asian populations have lower rates of common diseases and symptoms, such as heart disease, cancer, and menopausal symptoms, when compared with populations in the West.

Since the benefits of soy foods have been recognized in countries outside Asia they have surged in popularity, with annual sales of over $2 billion in the United States alone. This figure is undoubtedly due in part to the U.S. Food and Drug Administration's decision to approve a health claim based on the role of soy protein in reducing heart disease.

The heart

Heart disease is a major health concern because it causes more deaths in the West than any other disease. Soy foods can form part of a heart-friendly diet, as a high intake of soy products is associated with a lower incidence and reduced risk of heart disease. Research has found that regular consumption of soy can reduce the risk of heart disease by 10 percent for people who are at low risk and as much as 40 percent for people at high risk.

Soy protein is the component thought to be responsible for these benefits. Studies indicate that soy protein reduces total and low-density lipoprotein (LDL) cholesterol: the "bad cholesterol" that builds up inside the arteries, narrowing them and consequently reducing blood flow.

These findings have resulted in the U.S. Food and Drug Administration permitting soy products to be labeled with the following health claim regarding heart disease: "Diets low in saturated fat and cholesterol that include 25 grams of soy protein a day may reduce the risk of heart disease."

The 25 grams of soy protein needed to obtain the cholesterol-lowering benefits equal two to three servings of soy protein foods a day. The following list gives the soy protein contents of some common soy foods:

4 oz (125 g) firm tofu	20 g soy protein
4 oz (125 g) soft or silken tofu	9 g soy protein
1 soy-based burger	10–12 g soy protein
1 cup (8 fl oz/250 ml) plain soy drink	7 g soy protein
1 soy protein bar	14 g soy protein
1/2 cup (3 1/2 oz/105 g) cooked soybeans	18 g soy protein
1/2 cup (2 3/4 oz/80 g) tempeh	19 g soy protein
1/2 cup (1 3/4 oz/50 g) roasted soy nuts	19 g soy protein

In addition to soy protein, soy products also contain soluble fiber and unsaturated fats, which also help to reduce the risk of heart disease.

Cancer

The phytoestrogens, specifically the isoflavones, in soy products are thought to play a role in reducing the risk of cancer, in particular breast, colon and prostate cancer.

People living in Asia generally have lower rates of these diseases. In fact, the risk of Japanese women developing breast cancer is four to five times lower than it is for women in the West.

Human studies are currently inconclusive with regards to the effects of phytoestrogens on cancer risk, although animal studies are more promising. However, it is difficult to extrapolate these results to humans, so further research in this area is warranted.

Menopause

Cross-cultural studies have sparked an interest in the relationship between soy products and menopause. Asian women, who consume more soy foods compared to women living in the West, report fewer menopausal symptoms such as hot flashes (flushes).

Early studies showed that certain dietary phytoestrogens can exert mild estrogenic effects in post-menopausal women; however, subsequent research has not been consistent. Because of that, it is somewhat premature to recommend soy foods as a treatment for menopausal symptoms, although there is minimal risk in doing so.

Osteoporosis

Many factors contribute to the risk of osteoporosis, including genetics, imbalance of hormones, poor diet and lack of weight-bearing exercise.

Calcium is a major dietary protector against osteoporosis, and choosing calcium-fortified soy products like fortified soy milk and tofu can help provide adequate calcium to reduce the risk of low bone density and consequently of osteoporosis.

Furthermore, soy products provide other components that may be beneficial for maximizing bone density. Emerging evidence linking the role of phytoestrogens to bone health is increasing, although more human trials are needed to strengthen this association. Some research has also looked at the effects of soy protein on bone loss, but the research is inconclusive to date.

Weight control

Because of their relatively low calorie (kilojoule) content and their high fiber content, soy foods such as soybeans, tofu, tempeh and low-fat soy beverages can form part of a well-balanced diet for weight control.

Allergies

Some people suffer from food allergies or intolerances. However, once offending foods have been identified and eliminated from the diet, it is of paramount importance that other food sources replace the missing nutrients. In many instances, soy products can help people maintain an adequate nutrient intake by replacing the foods that initiate allergies.

Lactose intolerance

Many people have difficulty and discomfort digesting lactose, which is the main type of sugar found in dairy products, including milk (cow, goat, sheep and human), yogurt, some cheeses and ice cream. Of all the dairy products, milk is the major dietary contributor of lactose.

There are several health consequences associated with the inadequate intake of and ability to digest lactose. While lactose intolerance can lead to diarrhea, dehydration and eventual malnutrition if left unchecked, individuals who consume little or no lactose may also have low dietary calcium intakes, which can result in an increased risk of osteoporosis.

Avoiding lactose-containing foods will alleviate the symptoms of intolerance. Important foods to avoid are: milk (cow, goat, sheep and human); yogurt without live cultures; buttermilk; ice cream; cream cheese; milk chocolate; milk-based drink flavorings; commercial or homemade foods containing milk, milk solids, whey or lactose.

Soy products can be a great alternative to these foods because most contain no lactose. For example, a calcium-fortified soy beverage can replace milk in your diet if you are lactose intolerant, although labels should always be checked before purchase.

The nutritional value of soy

Nutritionally, soybeans are high in quality protein, low in saturated fat and high in fiber, and contain no cholesterol. They also supply essential fats, vitamins and minerals, and are the richest known source of the antioxidants called phytoestrogens.

Protein

Protein is composed of amino acids, which are the building blocks for the body. Growth and development depend on the presence of protein. Repair and maintenance of all tissues in the body also require protein.

In the United States, the recommended daily protein intake for adults is 50 grams. The Australian recommendation is similar, at 0.75 grams per kilogram of body weight for adults (that is, 56 g for a 165-lb/75-kg male and 49 g for a 143-lb/65-kg female). Children, adolescents and very active people may require as much as 2 grams per kilogram of body weight per day to meet the specific needs of growth or strenuous exercise.

Animal sources of protein, such as lean meats, poultry, fish, eggs and dairy products, provide high-quality protein, thus supplying all of the essential amino acids that cannot be produced by the body. Plant sources are usually lacking one of these essential amino acids and are termed incomplete protein foods. Soybeans are an exception to this rule, providing all the essential amino acids, which makes them a very good substitute for meat.

Not only do soybeans contain the array of amino acids otherwise found only in animal sources, they also are a rich source of protein. Cooked soybeans provide 30–37 grams of protein per cup (7 oz/220 g), which is almost 50 percent of the daily requirement for an average adult female. Other legumes, such as red kidney beans, lima beans and lentils, provide only half this amount.

Soy protein is also different from other proteins from both animal and plant sources in that it has been shown to reduce total and LDL cholesterol levels.

While soybeans, soy beverages, tofu and soy flour all provide soy protein, it is important to remember that soy sauce and soybean oil contain no protein.

Phytoestrogens

Phytoestrogens are naturally occurring compounds that have a structure very similar to human estrogen, yet have a much weaker effect in the body. One class of phytoestrogens is called isoflavones, and these are found in the highest quantity in soybeans. The two types of isoflavones found in soybeans are genistein and daidzein.

Phytoestrogens are thought to play a role in reducing cancer risk, in particular of breast, colon and prostate cancer. This belief is due to the low incidence of these diseases in Asian populations who consume soybeans regularly.

Although phytoestrogen supplements are available, they are not recommended as an alternative to soy products because their safety has not been assessed. In addition, it is preferable to obtain all the nutritional benefits of soy products—including fiber, vitamins and minerals—rather than a concentrated dose of phytoestrogens in a pill.

Fats

The benefits of a low-fat diet are well documented. It is well accepted that excess total dietary fat contributes to obesity, and that a diet high in saturated fats is linked to heart disease, some cancers, diabetes and other lifestyle diseases. However, it has also been established that some fats are essential to provide the body with fat-soluble vitamins and essential fatty acids, both of which are beneficial for health. Two types of fats that must be supplied by the diet are the omega-3 fats, which provide linolenic acid, and the omega-6 fats, which provide linoleic acid.

Omega-3 fats are found in fish and fish oil, and in plant sources like soybeans. Omega-3s are necessary for heart health (they help prevent atherosclerosis and thrombosis), and they may also be important for fighting cancer and such inflammatory conditions as rheumatoid arthritis and inflammatory bowel disease, strengthening immune function, and assisting with brain development. Omega-6 fats are much more abundant in the diet and are provided by vegetable oils (including soybean oil), grains, nuts, seeds and wheat germ. Omega-6 fats help to regulate blood pressure and blood clotting, and are necessary for healthy cell membranes.

Omega-3 and omega-6 fats are polyunsaturated. Together with monounsaturated fat, these should make up the majority of the dietary fat consumed, with saturated fat kept to a minimum. While saturated fat has a negative effect on cholesterol levels, unsaturated fats have a positive or neutral effect.

Soybeans contain 17–20 grams of fat per cup (7 oz/220 g, cooked). Although this is more than other legumes supply, it is similar to the amount of fat found in lean red meat. And while the fat in meat is saturated, the type of fat in soybeans is predominantly unsaturated, and it contains both omega-3 and omega-6 essential fats.

Calcium

Calcium is essential for growth and for strengthening the bones. It is also important for nerve and muscle function. In the United States, the recommended daily intake is 1,000 mg. Australia recommends an intake of 800 mg per day for adults, with increased needs for postmenopausal, pregnant and lactating women, as well as for children and adolescents.

Dairy products are the best source, providing high levels of calcium that is easily absorbed. Soybeans, in comparison, are a moderate source of calcium, providing 167–224 mg per cup (7 oz/220 g, cooked). When used to make a soy beverage, only 10–32 mg of calcium per cup (8 fl oz/250 ml) remain. However, many soy drinks today are fortified with calcium, which increases the calcium content to up to 290–300 mg per cup (whole milk provides 294 mg per cup), making fortified soy drinks a great alternative to milk, especially for vegans and individuals with milk allergies or lactose intolerance.

Soluble fiber

Dietary fiber has many important functions, including keeping the bowel and digestive systems healthy and controlling cholesterol and weight. In the United States, it is recommended that adults consume 25 grams of dietary fiber each day. In Australia, 30 grams are recommended.

Soybeans are a very good source of dietary fiber, supplying 13 grams—more than one-third of the daily requirement—in every cup (7 oz/220 g, cooked). The type of fiber found predominantly in legumes, including soybeans, is soluble fiber. This type of fiber is important for slowing digestion to maximize the absorption of nutrients and for helping to regulate blood glucose and control satiety (the feeling of fullness). Soluble fiber also helps to lower total cholesterol levels by decreasing cholesterol absorption.

Vitamins and minerals

Not only do soy foods contain protein, dietary fiber, phytoestrogens and essential fats, but they also contain vitamins and minerals. Soybeans provide more of the following nutrients per cup than other legumes:

iron, which helps prevent fatigue

zinc, which improves immune function, growth and development

B vitamins, which are involved in energy production

magnesium, which is important for muscle contraction and the release of energy.

Tempeh, made from fermented soybeans, also provides vitamin B_{12}, while sprouted soybeans are a good source of vitamin C.

The iron in plant foods is not absorbed by the body as easily as that from animal sources, but absorption is enhanced by consuming foods that are rich in vitamin C along with the soy. Zinc absorption can be enhanced by combining soy foods with some form of animal protein, such as dairy products, eggs and meats.

Energy

Energy is essential to fuel the body, but consuming more calories (kilojoules) than we need will result in weight gain.

Soybeans are a relatively low-energy food, providing only 283–381 calories (1186–1593 kj) per cup (7 oz/220 g, cooked). Similarly, tofu is also low in energy, providing 23–44 calories (187 kj) per 1 oz (30 g)—62 percent fewer calories than the equivalent quantity of meat. This makes soy a useful food to incorporate into the diet when trying to control body weight.

Carbohydrates

Carbohydrates are the macronutrient responsible for providing fuel for the muscles and the brain to function optimally. Like meat, soybeans are a relatively poor source of carbohydrates; however, combining soybeans and soy products with rice, noodles, couscous or potatoes can create a well-balanced, carbohydrate-rich meal.

The glycemic index (GI) of a food is a ranking of the effect that the food has on blood glucose levels. Low-GI foods result in a small but continuous rise in blood glucose levels. Such foods are important for controlling blood glucose levels in people with diabetes, and they are also good for weight control because of their high satiety value. In this case, soybeans are a great choice, as they have a very low GI of 18.

How much soy do we need?

Soy foods can be considered an exchange for the meat and meat-alternatives food group, and also forms part of the dairy group (fortified soy products can be used as an exchange for milk, cheese and yogurt).

Vegetables, legumes

The requirement for this category is a minimum of 5 servings per day. One-half cup (3 1/2 oz/105 g) of cooked soybeans is equivalent to one serving of vegetables.

Milk, cheese, yogurt

The requirement for this category is a minimum of 2 servings per day. One serving of milk is equivalent to 1 cup (8 fl oz/250 ml) of calcium-fortified soy milk; one serving of cheese is equivalent to 1 1/2 oz (45 g) of calcium-fortified soy cheese; one serving of yogurt is equivalent to 7–8 oz (220–250 g) of calcium-fortified soy yogurt.

Meat, fish, poultry, eggs, nuts, legumes

The requirement for this category is a minimum of 1 serving per day. One serving of legumes is equivalent to 1/2 cup (3 1/2 oz/105 g) of cooked soybeans.

Soy products have advanced to the forefront of the Western marketplace only over the last decade. Much of this explosion in the market has been due to research revealing that soy products are more beneficial for our health than we had previously thought.

The health benefits associated with soy products involve conditions and symptoms that can affect individuals at any time in their lifespan, so it is never too early to "get into soy." The problem some individuals have faced of how to prepare, use and consume soy products can be easily solved with the many products that are available on our supermarket shelves. These may be modified versions of the basic soybean, but they make it easy to incorporate soy into healthy and delicious meals.

With an increased understanding of how to use soy and include it in your daily eating plan, you can be confident in knowing that these products are providing your body with an excellent source of important nutrients. Furthermore, these foods do not need to replace the foods you already eat, but they can easily complement your existing diet.

How to use the Nutrition Table

The table across shows the nutritional value of various soy products. The first listing in the table (dark green) refers to products found in the U.S. The second listing (light green) refers to products found in Australia. Simply look up the food that you eat and check the energy, protein, fat, and carbohydrate value as well as the amount of fiber and calcium supplied in one serve.

The measurements used in the table are the same as those used throughout the book. See page 111 for the Guide to Weights and Measures.

Nutrition Table credits: The U.S. food listings (dark green) are from the USDA nutrient database (www.nal.usda.gov/fnic/cgi-bin/nut_search.pl).
The Australian food listings (light green) are from the nutritional database of Australian food: Nuttab95, Australian Government Publishing Service, 1995; and from Rogers, J. (1990), What Food is That? and How Healthy is It?, Lansdowne Publishing.

Nutrition Table

Soy product	Amount	Energy Kj	Energy Cals	Protein g	Fat g	Carbohydrate g	Fiber g	Calcium mg
Soybeans, boiled	1 cup (7 oz)	1593	381	37	20	22	13	224
Soybeans, boiled	1 cup (220 g)	1186	283	30	17	3	16	167
Soy beverage, fortified	1 cup (8 fl oz)	545	130	6	4	N/A	N/A	300
Soy beverage, fortified	1 cup (250 ml)	650	155	9	9	12	1	290
Soy beverage, unfortified	1 cup (8 fl oz)	345	83	7	5	5	3	10
Soy beverage, unfortified	1 cup (250 ml)	410	98	6	5	6	1	32
Tofu, firm, calcium fortified	1 oz	182	44	5	3	1	1	205
Tofu, firm, calcium fortified	30 g	87	23	2	1	1	0	150
Soybean oil	1 tbsp (1/2 fl oz)	555	133	0	15	0	0	0
Soybean oil	1 tbsp (15 ml)	527	126	0	14	0	0	0
Miso	1 tbsp (15 g)	129	31	2	1	4	1	10
Miso	1 tbsp (15 g)	106	25	2	1	4	N/A	N/A
Soy flour	1 cup (5 oz)	2,827	676	54	32	55	15	319
Soy flour	1 cup (150 g)	2,666	636	53	32	35	20	318
Soy flour, low fat	1 cup (5 oz)	2,412	577	72	10	59	16	291
Soy flour, low fat	1 cup (150 g)	2,248	537	72	10	39	24	291

Soybeans

Green Soybeans, Fresh and Frozen

Green soybeans, which are harvested when young and immature, and are known by the Japanese name *edamame*, are only occasionally available fresh, but they are readily available frozen, both in the pod and shelled, from Asian food stores. Boiled in lightly salted water until tender for 5–10 minutes, these can be eaten straight from the pods like broad beans, as a side dish, or in soup or pasta.

Dried Soybeans

Dried soybeans are readily available in western supermarkets and natural foods stores. There are many varieties, but the most common are the beige and the black. Soaking and cooking times may vary depending on the age of the beans, but lengthy cooking is necessary to destroy their trypsin inhibitors, which prevent the body from absorbing the soy's protein. The rich, creamy texture and taste of cooked soybeans is similar to that of chestnuts. They can be enjoyed very simply, with a splash of soy sauce and a few scallions (shallots/spring onions) or tossed with some Asian sesame oil and garlic. Black soybeans are available dried in bags or vacuum-sealed packs or salted in cans. Rinse salted soybeans well before use.

How to Buy and Prepare Soybeans

Selecting and storing dried soybeans
Properly dried and stored, soybeans should have smooth, shiny and intact skins, with few broken or skinless beans in the packet. Keep dried soybeans in an airtight container.

Preparing dried soybeans
Pick over the beans and remove any that are discolored, along with any foreign matter. Rinse the beans under cold water. One cup (7 oz/220 g) dried soybeans makes about 2^1/2 cups (17^1/2 oz/545 g) cooked. A 10-oz (300-g) can of

soybeans is the equivalent of $^1/_2$ cup ($3^1/_2$ oz/105 g) dried soybeans, soaked and cooked.

Soaking

Soaking dried soybeans before cooking not only shortens the cooking time, but ensures even cooking and improves digestibility. Put dried soybeans in a large bowl and cover with lightly salted water (the salt helps keep the delicate skins intact). Cover and refrigerate for 6–8 hours, or overnight, if convenient. Drain and rinse the beans, discarding any loose skins. The soaking water can be reserved and used for stock or soup; it can be refrigerated for up to 3 days or frozen for up to 6 months.

Pan-roasting

Dried soybeans need no soaking if they are pan-roasted before cooking. Place rinsed soybeans in a large frying pan and place it over high heat, stirring the beans constantly. The skins will dry and begin to shrivel, then become smooth again and split open in 3–4 minutes. Turn the heat off and continue stirring for a minute longer. Remove the beans from the pan and allow to cool before cooking.

Boiling

Rinse soaked dried soybeans and drain them. Put the beans in a large saucepan and add enough water to cover the beans by about 1 inch (2.5 cm), about 4 cups (32 fl oz/1 L) for every cup (7 oz/220 g) of beans. Bring to a boil, reduce heat and simmer, covered, until tender, 2–3 hours. Occasionally remove any scum from the surface and add water as required to keep the beans covered. Some Japanese chefs also add a type of seaweed, konbu, which is believed to make the beans more digestible. The amount added depends on the quantity of the soybeans cooked.

Dried soybeans can also be cooked unsoaked, but they will require at least 3 hours cooking to become tender.

The cooking water can be reserved and used for stock or soup. Cooked soybeans and the cooking liquid can be refrigerated, separately, for up to 3 days or frozen for up to 6 months.

Pressure cooking

Using a pressure cooker can reduce the cooking time for both soaked and unsoaked dried soybeans dramatically, from 2–3 hours to 30–35 minutes, and the result is tender and creamy textured beans.

Place the beans into the pressure cooker and cover with lightly salted water. Slowly bring to a boil, uncovered, over medium-high heat, removing any foam or scum from the surface. Reduce heat to a simmer and add any extra ingredients such as konbu, onion or garlic. Cover the pressure cooker and cook according to the manufacturer's instructions until the beans are tender, about 35 minutes.

Canned

If time is short, cooked beige soybeans are readily available from supermarkets in cans of various sizes. Drain and rinse the beans before use.

Salted

Rinse salted soybeans well before adding 1–2 tablespoons to stir-fries or sauces. These beans combine well with ginger, garlic and other Asian flavors.

Soy Foods

Tofu

Tofu, also known as bean curd, is a white soybean curd made by curdling fresh hot soy milk with a coagulant. Rich in protein and very versatile, it is available from supermarkets, fresh, in vaccum-sealed packs as well as in shelf-stable cartons or long-life packages. Whether tofu is extra-firm, firm or soft is determined by how much liquid is extracted from the curds. The firmer the tofu the more protein it contains. Organic tofu is also available.

Selecting and using tofu

Generally, firm, silken firm and extra-firm tofu is best for stir-fries, kebabs, or dishes that require tofu to hold its shape (see Mini Sweet Soy Chicken Balls, page 30) for crumbling or grating. Silken firm and fresh tofu will puree well. Chinese-style tofu is usually firmer and coarser than the softer, more delicate Japanese-style tofu. Nigari tofu is firm, and gets its name from the traditional Japanese coagulant that is used to make it, which is considered to give tofu the best flavor.

Silken soft tofu and soft tofu have a soft and creamy texture. They can hold their shape if handled very carefully. Silken firm, silken soft, soft and fresh tofu can be readily pureed for dips, salad dressings, drinks, sauces and to replace some dairy products, such as sour cream, in dishes.

Silken tofu differs from soft tofu in its preparation method. The texture of silken tofu depends on the amount of coagulant and the thickness of the soy milk used. The tofu is not drained so the curds and whey are not separated. The resulting tofu has a slightly higher water content and will not therefore absorb flavors readily. Silken tofu is particularly suitable on its own with a sauce or added to soups.

Flavored tofu (such as mango, coconut, almond and pandan) can be served as a dessert with fresh fruit or pureed as a dessert topping.

Storing

Shelf-stable tofu requires no refrigeration until opened. Keep fresh tofu and shelf-stable tofu, once opened, covered with water and refrigerated in an airtight container. Change the water daily, and use the tofu within 2–5 days, depending on manufacturers' instructions. Discard any tofu that smells sour or has darkened around the edges.

Freezing

Tofu can be frozen, but the color and texture will change. Freezing silken or soft tofu is not recommended as the soft creamy texture is ruined. Frozen tofu can be defrosted quickly in the microwave or in the refrigerator overnight. Drain and press defrosted tofu to expel any excess liquid before use. Defrosted tofu is darker in color than fresh tofu, has a chewier, coarser, open texture and absorbs flavors like a sponge.

Tofu

Bean curd sheets (yuba)

Deep-fried tofu

Deep-fried tofu pouches: Seasoned tofu

Miso

Tempeh

Top to bottom: Ketjap manis, tamari, light soy sauce

Soy milk

Soy flour

Soy nuts

Soy germ powder

Soy oil

Soybean sprouts

Soybean paste

Soy dairy products: spread, yogurt, cheese

Soy meats

Soy chocolate, bread, flavored tofu and pasta

Bean Curd Sheets (Yuba)

Sheets of dried bean curd are made from the skin that forms on the surface when soy milk is heated. Creamy, sweet and delicious when freshly made, they are high in protein and contain no saturated fats or cholesterol. Available dried or frozen from Asian food stores, they can be used as a wrap, added to soups, deep-fried, panfried, baked or steamed.

Deep-Fried Tofu (Age)

Large or small diced deep-fried tofu (tofu puffs) or thickly sliced (atsuage) or thinly sliced (aburaage) tofu can be added to stir-fries and casseroles. Thinly sliced tofu can be opened and stuffed with sweet or savory fillings. Pour boiling water over deep-fried tofu to remove excess oil, then squeeze gently to remove excess water before use. Deep-fried tofu is available refrigerated or frozen from Asian food stores.

Seasoned tofu

Thinly sliced deep-fried tofu pouches seasoned with sweet soy are traditionally filled with sushi rice or added to stir-fries and rice dishes. It is available in refrigerated packets or canned from Asian food stores. Once opened, use seasoned tofu within 3–4 days, or freeze it for up to 3 months.

Miso

This salty, high-protein paste is made from fermented soybeans, sometimes mixed with other cereal grains, like rice and barley. As a general rule, the darker the color (red and brown miso), the saltier the taste, and the lighter the color (white shiro, and yellow miso), the sweeter the taste. Miso is available in refrigerated packs and resealable tubs. Organic and salt-reduced misos are also available from Asian and natural foods stores. Miso can be kept refrigerated in an airtight container for more than 1 year.

Tempeh

Tempeh consists of hulled, cooked soybeans that are fermented and bound together in cakes by a white mold (mycelium), similar to that on soft, ripened cheeses. It is readily available, plain or seasoned, in refrigerated packs. Once opened, use tempeh within 5 days, or freeze it for up to 3 months. It can be marinated, pureed, grilled, fried or steamed, as well as sliced, diced, crumbled or pureed. As tempeh absorbs oil easily, brush or spray pieces lightly with oil and fry it in a nonstick pan.

Soy Sauce (Shoyu)

Soy sauce is made from fermented soybeans and is used to enhance the flavor of many dishes, both sweet and savory. Keep refrigerated once opened and use within 12 months.

Different types of soy sauce have different tastes and degrees of saltiness. Chinese soy sauce is saltier and stronger in taste than the Japanese style and should not be used in delicately flavored dishes. Buy only good-quality soy sauce, as the cheaper brands are made quickly with artificial flavors and colorings.

Regular soy sauce

Regular soy sauce is naturally brewed and has a rich flavor and dark color. It is often made with the addition of wheat. Mushroom soy, and seasoned soy sauces (such as teriyaki sauce with Chinese five-spice powder, and roasted garlic) are also available.

Low-salt soy sauce

Nearly half the salt is removed from original soy sauce, after the brewing process, to make low-salt soy sauce.

Light soy sauce

Light soy sauce is lighter in color but slightly saltier in taste than regular soy sauce and is used to avoid darkening sauces or salad dressings.

Tamari

Tamari is a thick, dark soy sauce. Because the soybeans are brewed without the addition of wheat, tamari contains no wheat gluten, making it especially suitable for people with wheat allergies or celiac disease.

Ketjap manis

Also known as kecap manis, this thick Indonesian soy sauce is sweetened with palm sugar. Available in sweet or semi-sweet varieties, it is versatile and especially suitable for use with tempeh, to brush on deep-fried tofu and stir-fries.

Soy Milk

Soy milk is an excellent cholesterol- and lactose-free alternative to dairy milk. It is available in refrigerated packages or shelf-stable cartons that require no refrigeration until opened. It comes in many styles, including thickened, fat-reduced, fat-free, fortified with calcium or vitamins, with added soy and linseed or sweetened or flavored. Use it within 5 days.

Soy milk can replace dairy milk in most recipes but is slightly darker in color, has a mild, nutty flavor and will curdle if boiled.

Soy Flour

Because soy flour does not contain any gluten as wheat flour does, it can only be used for baking in small amounts or the food will not rise. It can be mixed with other flours for general baking or added to soy drinks with soy milk and/or tofu. Because of its shorter shelf life, it should be kept refrigerated in an airtight container.

Soy Nuts

Like peanuts, these nuts are available from Asian and natural foods stores. To make your own, soak dried soybeans in cold water for about 3 hours to soften. Drain and place them on a lightly greased baking sheet lined with parchment (baking) paper, and bake in a preheated 350°F (180°C) oven, turning every few minutes, until well browned, about 20 minutes.

Soy Germ Powder

To make soy germ powder, the soy germ (the nucleus of the soy kernel) is roasted and ground to a fine powder.

This concentrated form of soy protein can be added to virtually any foods, such as sauces, drinks or dips, or sprinkled on cereal to increase their protein content.

Soy Oil

Once refined, the light-colored oil extracted from whole soybeans has a neutral taste and can be used as an all-purpose cooking or salad oil.

Soybean Sprouts

A common ingredient in stir-fries and many Chinese dishes, soybean sprouts have a coarser texture and stronger flavor than other bean sprouts. Although they can be used raw in salads, many people prefer to blanch them for 1–2 minutes. The sprouts consist of the green bean, the cream-colored stem and a stringy tail. Finished dishes will look better if the stringy tails have been removed. Use the sprouts as a garnish or sauté them quickly in stir-fries. They are available fresh from supermarkets and produce stores. Store in the refrigerator for 4–5 days and discard them if they become soft or watery.

Soybean Paste

Pastes and sauces made from fermented soybeans, often combined with garlic, chili and vinegar, are available in jars from Asian food stores. Panfry the paste with meat or vegetables or add it to sauces or soups to enhance flavor. Refrigerate after opening.

Natto

Made from steamed, fermented and mashed soybeans, natto's glutinous and slimy texture and strong cheeselike flavor is an acquired taste for Westerners. More easily digested than whole soybeans, natto is used as a flavoring and table condiment, especially in Japan, where it is served over rice for breakfast. It can be mixed with other ingredients, such as mustard, soy sauce and chives, and used as a salad dressing.

Soy Dairy Products

Soy butter, soy spread (margarine), plain or flavored soy cheese, cream cheese, yogurt and mayonnaise are available at selected supermarkets and natural foods stores. Most are lactose- and cholesterol-free, although labels should be checked as the products vary with different manufacturers. Most can be substituted for their dairy equivalent in recipes. Soy butter and margarine can be used for general baking and as spreads, but the butter does not melt, so use soy margarine or oil instead. Soy cheese has a mild flavor, but does not brown or melt well.

Soy Meats

Meat alternatives made from soybeans, such as soy hamburgers and cutlets, look, taste and are cooked like the meat they replace. They are available frozen, refrigerated or dried from natural foods stores and some supermarkets.

Others

The number of soy foods appearing on the market is increasing constantly. Some are nutritionally better than others, depending on the other ingredients added, so always check the labels before buying. Soy breads, cereals, pasta, chocolate, chips, health bars, desserts and tofu ice cream are available in natural foods stores and some supermarkets.

Soy Grits
Soy grits are dried soybeans that have been lightly toasted, then cracked into small pieces. They can replace some flour in recipes or be added to salads such as tabbouleh or other dishes to increase the protein content. Soy grits should be soaked before use.

Tips

Tofu
Once opened, keep tofu refrigerated and covered with water that is changed daily. Use it within 2–5 days, depending on manufacturers' instructions.

The textures and flavors of tofu vary among brands. For instance, some firm tofu is very firm and crumbles or grates well, while other firm tofu is soft enough to puree smoothly.

Although all tofu can be cut into decorative shapes, silken and soft tofu must be handled very carefully or it will break.

Always drain and press tofu (see page 24) to remove excess liquid before deep-frying or pan-frying or the oil will spatter.

Longer pressing, grilling or gently boiling for 2 minutes will firm the texture of tofu—a quick fix to turn soft tofu into firm.

Tofu can provide moisture and structure to baked dishes without altering their flavor. Be sure the tofu is pureed until smooth before adding it to baked dishes or the tofu bits will harden as they cook, giving the food an unappetizing look and taste.

Substitute about 1/4 cup (2 fl oz/60 ml) pureed silken tofu for each egg in pancake, muffin, quick bread and cake recipes, or reduce the number of eggs used by replacing half the eggs with tofu.

Soy dairy products
Most soy dairy products (milk, butter, cheese) can be substituted for their dairy equivalent in recipes.

The thickness, sweetness and fat content of soy milks, drinks and yogurts varies among brands, so check labels before purchase.

Compatible Soy Flavors

What flavors go with soy foods? Fortunately, just about any, sweet or savory. Soy foods are remarkably versatile and combine well with many readily available ingredients and flavors, whether Asian, Mediterranean, Moroccan or Indian. Many of the ingredients listed in this section can be found in delicatessens, natural foods stores and supermarkets. Others are well worth the effort to seek them out from specialty foods stores.

Oils

Ghee, olive oil, peanut oil, Asian sesame oil.

Herbs and Spices

Basil, cayenne, chili, Chinese five-spice powder, chives, cilantro (fresh coriander), cumin, curry leaves and powder, garlic, ginger, kaffir lime leaves, lemongrass, mint, Szechuan pepper, tamarind, Thai basil, turmeric, umeboshi (Japanese sour plum).

Herbs and spices (clockwise left to right): Cilantro (fresh coriander), ginger, orange zest, garlic

Stocks, Sauces and Seasoning

Black and white sesame seeds, Shaoxing wine, coconut milk or cream, dashi (made with konbu seaweed and bonito fish flakes; instant dashi granules are available in Asian food stores), hoisin sauce, Indian chutneys and relishes, ketjap manis (sweet soy sauce), mirin, miso, nam pla (fermented fish sauce), Parmesan cheese, preserved lemons, oyster sauce, plum sauce, rice vinegar, sake, sambal oelek (red chili paste), shrimp paste, soy sauce, sweet chili sauce, tamarind pulp, wasabi paste, Worcestershire sauce.

Fruits and Vegetables

Kaffir limes, lemons (including preserved lemons), limes, oranges, scallions (shallots/spring onions), shiitake mushrooms (fresh and dried), tomatoes, onions.

Noodles

Egg noodles, fresh and dried rice noodles, mung bean noodles (cellophane), soba and green tea soba noodles, somen, udon.

Others

Nori and other seaweeds.

Herbs and vegetables (left to right): Mint, tomato, red chili peppers

Noodles (left to right): Dried somen, soba, udon

Preparation and Cooking Techniques

Draining and Pressing Tofu

Tofu should be drained in a colander before use to prevent excess liquid spattering when it is fried or diluting sauces it is cooked with. Pressing tofu before use makes it firmer and even less watery and allows it to better absorb flavors from marinades and sauces. Many dishes only require a gentle push with the hand to expel liquid, but if the tofu is to be deep-fried, it should be wrapped in paper towels and left with 2 dinner plates placed on top for at least 15 minutes, or longer for a drier, firmer texture. Alternatively, place tofu between 2 tilted cutting boards with a weight on top and leave to drain into the sink for at least 15 minutes. Pat tofu dry before cooking.

How to drain tofu
Step 1: Wrap tofu in paper towels and let stand with 1 or 2 dinner plates on top.

Hard and soft tofu

24

Cutting Tofu

Although all tofu can be sliced, diced or cut into decorative shapes with biscuit cutters, silken and soft tofu must be handled very carefully or it will break.

Deep-Frying Tofu

Deep-frying tofu slices and puffs can be an alternative to buying ready-made deep-fried tofu. First, drain and press firm tofu, then slice, dice or cut it into triangles and deep-fry. For a crisper texture, lightly coat tofu in cornstarch (cornflour) or potato flour, which can be seasoned with chili pepper flakes, curry powder or sesame seeds, or dip tofu in lightly beaten egg and then in bread crumbs before deep-frying or panfrying.

How to Reconstitute Yuba

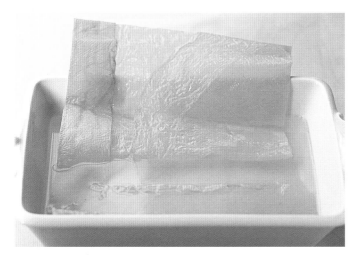

Step 1: Place a sheet of bean curd (yuba) in a shallow bowl of warm water. Soak for 10–20 seconds.

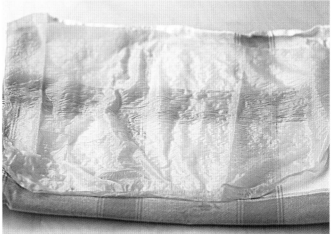

Step 2: When the bean curd sheet is reconstituted (soft and pliable), place it on a cloth and pat it dry.

How to Use Deep-fried Tofu Pouches

Step 1: Pour boiling water over deep-fried tofu pouches (or simmer for 1 minute in boiling water) to remove excess oil.

Step 2: When tofu is cool enough, squeeze out excess liquid. Pat dry with paper towels.

Step 3: Cut large pieces of tofu (5-inch/13-cm) in half to make 2 pouches. Trim smaller tofu on long side to make an opening.

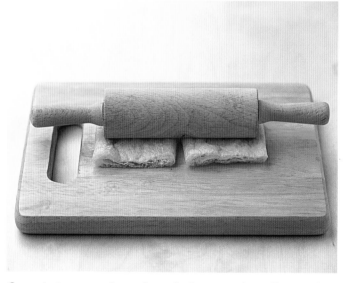

Step 4: Lay pouch on board, then gently roll it with a rolling pin to break fibers inside and make easier to open.

How to Use Miso

Cooking with miso

Experimenting with the type and amount of miso to use in recipes—from the slightly sweet, less salty light miso to the rich, complex, saltier dark miso—can be fun. Use one or a combination of different types of miso as a condiment, in soups, sauces, salad dressings, marinades and casseroles, with vegetables or even on toast.

The saltiness varies for each type and brand, so always start with less than a recipe calls for and then add more as needed. As a guide, 1 tablespoon of light or 2 teaspoons of dark miso per cup (8 fl oz/250 ml) of water or stock provides a good flavor base. Before adding miso into a hot dish, mix it in a cup with enough hot liquid to make a smooth paste to avoid lumps.

Miso: Tips

Add less miso to a dish than a recipe calls for, as saltiness can vary with type and brand. Taste the dish and add more miso if required.

Miso is usually stirred in at the end of cooking so its flavor is not lost with high temperatures.

Step 1: To avoid lumps, mix miso with a small amount of the hot cooking liquid in a cup until mixture is smooth before adding it to pot.

Step 2: Gradually stir miso mixture into remaining hot liquid.

Soups

Leek and Fennel Soup with Tempeh Crisps

2 tablespoons soybean oil
2 cloves garlic, finely chopped
2 fennel bulbs (1 lb/500 g), trimmed and sliced
1 large leek, rinsed and sliced
1 lb (500 g) potatoes, peeled and sliced
4 cups (32 fl oz/1 L) chicken or vegetable stock
salt and cracked pepper to taste
5 oz (150 g) silken or soft tofu, drained
1 tablespoon finely chopped fresh chives

For tempeh crisps
2$^{1}/_{2}$ oz (75 g) tempeh
canola oil for deep-frying

In a large saucepan, heat oil over medium-low heat. Add garlic, fennel and leek and cook until leek begins to soften, 5–8 minutes. Add potatoes, stock, salt and pepper. Cover and simmer until vegetables are soft, 15–20 minutes. Strain soup, reserving liquid. In a food processor, puree vegetables with tofu until smooth. Return to saucepan with reserved liquid and simmer, without boiling, until heated through. Sprinkle with chives and tempeh crisps to serve.

To make crisps: Slice tempeh into matchsticks, about $^{1}/_{4}$ inch by $^{1}/_{4}$ inch (6 mm) wide and 1 inch (2.5 cm) long. Fill a wok or large frying pan one-third full with oil and heat to 365°F (185°C). Deep-fry tempeh until crisp, 1–2 minutes. Drain on paper towels. (Note: These can be made ahead and stored in an airtight container for 1–2 days.)

Herb and Tomato Soup with Parmesan Toasts

1 tablespoon soybean oil
1 onion, cut into thin wedges
1 clove garlic, crushed
1 stalk celery, chopped
1 carrot, chopped
14$^{1}/_{2}$ oz (455 g) canned tomatoes with herbs
$^{1}/_{4}$ cup (2 oz/60 g) tomato paste
10 oz (300 g) canned soybeans, drained
4 cups (32 fl oz/1 L) vegetable or chicken stock
2 tablespoons Worcestershire sauce
$^{1}/_{3}$ cup (1 oz/30 g) soy spiral pasta
10 mini tofu puffs
2 tablespoons finely chopped fresh basil
1 tablespoon finely chopped fresh oregano
1 small red chili pepper, seeded and finely chopped
2 tablespoons finely chopped fresh parsley

For Parmesan toasts
4 slices soy and linseed bread
vegetable-oil cooking spray
$^{1}/_{4}$ cup (1 oz/30 g) grated Parmesan cheese
1 tablespoon finely chopped fresh parsley

In a large saucepan, heat oil over medium heat and sauté onion and garlic until onion is soft, about 2 minutes. Add celery, carrot, tomatoes, tomato paste, soybeans, stock, Worcestershire sauce, pasta, tofu puffs, herbs and chili flakes. Bring to a boil, reduce heat, cover and simmer for 30 minutes (note: add more stock at this point if thinner consistency is preferred). Sprinkle with parsley and serve with Parmesan toasts.

To make Parmesan toasts: Preheat oven to 400°F (200°C). Remove crusts from bread and lightly spray each slice with cooking spray. Sprinkle slices with Parmesan and parsley, pressing lightly to make them stick. Cut slices into triangles. Place on a baking sheet and bake until lightly browned and crisp, about 10 minutes.

Miso Noodle Soup

3¹/₂ oz (105 g) dried somen noodles
6 cups (48 fl oz/1.5 L) water
2¹/₂ teaspoons dashi granules
1 cup (2 oz/60 g) soybean sprouts
¹/₃ cup (3 oz/90 g) red miso
3 scallions (shallots/spring onions) white and green parts, finely sliced
6¹/₂ oz (200 g) firm or soft tofu, cut into ¹/₂-inch (1-cm) cubes
shichimi (seven spices) or ¹/₂ small red chili pepper, seeded and finely chopped

Cut noodles into 4-inch (10-cm) lengths. In a saucepan of boiling water, add noodles and cook, uncovered, until just tender, about 5 minutes. Drain. In a medium saucepan, combine 6 cups (48 fl oz/1.5 L) water, dashi granules and soybean sprouts. Bring to a boil then reduce heat to a simmer. Put miso in a cup, add 1 tablespoon hot liquid and stir until smooth. Gradually stir miso into simmering soup. Add tofu cubes and white parts of scallions. Divide noodles among bowls and ladle in hot soup. Sprinkle with green parts of scallions and shichimi.
Serves 4–6

Right: Leek and Fennel Soup with Tempeh Crisps

Variations: In place of soybean sprouts, substitute strips of deep-fried tofu pouches, deep-fried tofu puffs, wakame (seaweed), snow pea sprouts, spinach, enoki or shiitake mushrooms or sliced daikon (white radish).

Substitute white miso for red; increase amount by 1 tablespoon or to taste.
Serves 4

Appetizers and Dips

Mini Sweet Soy Chicken Balls

13 oz (400 g) ground (minced) chicken
3¹/₂ oz (105 g) extra-firm or firm tofu, drained and shredded
4 scallions (shallots/spring onions), thinly sliced
1 clove garlic, crushed
2 tablespoons finely chopped fresh parsley
2 teaspoons red or white miso
2 teaspoons grated orange zest
¹/₄ teaspoon Chinese five-spice powder
¹/₂ cup (1 oz/30 g) day-old bread crumbs
¹/₄ cup (2 fl oz/60 ml) ketjap manis mixed with 1 tablespoon light soy sauce
vegetable-oil cooking spray
ketjap manis for serving

Preheat oven to 350°F (180°C). In a medium bowl, combine chicken, tofu, scallions, garlic, parsley, miso, orange zest, spice and bread crumbs. Mix well. Shape into 24 small balls, about 1¹/₂ inches (4 cm) in diameter. Roll each ball in ketjap manis mixture, allowing excess to drain off, then place on prepared baking sheet and bake until cooked through, 8–10 minutes. Serve immediately, with extra ketjap manis.

Makes 24

Variations: Toss cooked balls with hot rice noodles and extra ketjap manis and serve as a main course.

Substitute lamb for chicken.

Spicy Eggplant Dip

1 globe eggplant (aubergine), about 12 oz (375 g), peeled and diced
2 teaspoons salt
2 tablespoons soybean oil
1 clove garlic, finely chopped
3¹/₂ oz (105 g) silken firm or fresh tofu, drained
¹/₃ cup (3 oz/90 g) tahini (sesame paste)
¹/₄ cup (2 fl oz/60 ml) fresh lemon juice
1 tablespoon red miso
1 small red chili pepper, seeded and finely chopped (optional)
¹/₄ teaspoon paprika

Sprinkle eggplant with salt and let stand in a colander for 20 minutes. Rinse eggplant under cold water and pat dry with paper towels. In a medium frying pan, heat oil over medium-low heat and sauté eggplant and garlic until soft, about 10 minutes. In a food processor, combine eggplant, tofu, tahini, lemon juice and miso. Puree until smooth. Stir in chili pepper. If a thinner consistency is preferred, stir in some extra soybean oil.

Put mixture in a bowl, sprinkle with paprika and serve with tofu chips, Sesame Crackers (page 37) and crisp vegetable sticks.

Makes about 1¹/₂ cups (12 fl oz/375 ml)

Tip: The diced eggplant can also be brushed or sprayed with oil and baked in a preheated 400°F (200°C) oven until soft, about 15 minutes. The eggplant can also be baked whole until soft, about 40 minutes, then peeled and pureed.

Right: Mini Sweet Soy Chicken Balls

Massaman Curry Bites

2 tablespoons Massaman curry paste
2^1/$_2$ oz (75 g) white-fleshed fish, ground (minced)
2^1/$_2$ oz (75 g) firm or extra-firm tofu, drained and shredded
^{1}/$_3$ cup (^{2}/$_3$ oz/20 g) soybean sprouts, blanched and finely chopped
2 scallions (shallots/spring onions), finely chopped
1 tablespoon coconut milk
12 large deep-fried tofu puffs (5 oz/150 g)
^{1}/$_4$ cup (2 fl oz/60 ml) ketjap manis mixed with 1 tablespoon light soy sauce

Preheat oven to 400°F (180°C).

In a medium bowl, combine curry paste, fish, grated tofu, soybean sprouts, scallions and coconut milk. Cut each tofu puff in half diagonally and make a pocket inside with fingers. Fill each puff with about 1^1/$_2$ teaspoons of fish mixture. Brush outside of each puff, including filling, with ketjap manis mixture. Place filled puffs on a prepared baking sheet and bake until lightly browned and crisp, 8–10 minutes.

Makes 12

Tips: If using homemade tofu puffs, scoop inside out and add it to filling.

Adding soy sauce to ketjap manis lessens the sweetness of ketjap manis and thins the mixture for easier spreading.

Substitute red curry paste if Massaman curry is unavailable.

Tofu Chips

5 oz (150 g) firm or firm fresh tofu, drained and pressed (see page 24)
canola oil for deep-frying

Cut tofu into thin ^{1}/$_2$-inch (12-mm) slices. Pat dry with paper towels. Fill a wok or large frying pan one-third full with oil and heat to 365°F (185°C). Deep-fry tofu slices until golden brown and crunchy, 2–3 minutes. Drain on paper towels and let cool. Store in an airtight container for up to 2 days.

Seared Sashimi Tuna

1 lb (500 g) sashimi-grade tuna
2 teaspoons vegetable or canola oil
^{1}/$_4$ cup (2 fl oz/60 ml) Japanese soy sauce
^{1}/$_4$ cup (2 fl oz/60 ml) balsamic vinegar
2 scallions (shallots/spring onions), green parts only, finely sliced

Trim tuna and cut into steaks 1^1/$_2$ inches (4 cm) thick. Heat oil in a frying pan over high heat and sear tuna for 1 minute on each side for medium-rare. Immediately transfer tuna to a plate. Reduce heat to medium and heat soy sauce and balsamic vinegar in pan until thickened, 2–3 minutes. Return tuna to pan and turn carefully but quickly until well coated. Cut tuna into bite-sized pieces and serve warm or at room temperature with toothpicks, garnished with scallions.

Serves 6 as a finger food

Left: Massaman Curry Bites

Tomato Salsa in Toasted Soy Cups with Tofu, Avocado and Lime Cream

24 slices soy and linseed bread, crusts removed
vegetable-oil cooking spray
2 ripe tomatoes, seeded and finely diced
1/3 cup (1 1/2 oz/50 g) finely diced green bell pepper
(capsicum)
1 small red (Spanish) onion, finely chopped
1 teaspoon olive oil
1 teaspoon vinegar
1/2 teaspoon finely chopped green chili pepper (optional)
salt and cracked pepper to taste
cilantro (fresh coriander) leaves or mustard cress for garnish
Tofu, avocado and lime cream

Preheat oven to 400°F (200°C).

Flatten each bread slice with a rolling pin. Cut bread into 3-inch (8-cm) rounds using a biscuit (scone) cutter. Lightly spray both sides of bread slices with cooking spray and press them into muffin cups. Bake until lightly browned and crisp, about 10 minutes. Remove from oven and let cool.

Combine tomatoes, bell pepper, onion, oil, vinegar, chili, salt and pepper. Fill each cup with 2 teaspoons avocado and lime cream and 1 teaspoon salsa. Garnish with cilantro and serve immediately as cups will become soft if left standing.

Makes 24

Tip: Bread cases can be made a few days ahead and kept in an airtight container.

Tofu, Avocado and Lime Cream

4 oz (125 g) silken tofu, drained
2 teaspoons white (shiro) miso
4 teaspoons white vinegar
1 avocado, peeled, pitted and diced
salt and pepper to taste
1 1/2 tablespoons fresh lime juice
1 teaspoon each finely chopped fresh parsley, chives and mint

In food processor, process tofu until smooth. In a cup, combine 2 tablespoons of pureed tofu with miso and stir until smooth. Return tofu mixture to food processor and add all remaining ingredients. Process until well combined.

Makes 1 1/2 cups (12 fl oz/375 ml)

Variations: Serve tofu, avocado and lime cream as a dip with sesame crackers (page 37) and crisp vegetable sticks.

Use tofu, avocado and lime cream as a filling in wraps, savory pancakes or sandwiches.

Cut the top off steamed or baked whole potatoes and top with tofu, avocado and lime cream mixed with cooked crab meat.

Add tofu, avocado and lime cream to tacos and enchiladas.

Substitute wasabi paste for the chili pepper.

Right: Tomato Salsa
in Toasted Soy Cups with Tofu, Avocado and Lime Cream

Spicy Tahini Tofu with Sesame Crackers

For sesame crackers

1 tablespoon superfine (caster) sugar
2/3 cup (2 oz/60 g) white sesame seeds
2 teaspoons cracked pepper
2 tablespoons tahini (sesame paste)
1/2 cup (2 1/2 oz/75 g) all-purpose (plain) flour
1/4 cup (1 oz/30 g) soy flour
2 egg whites, lightly beaten
1/4 cup (2 fl oz/60 ml) Japanese soy sauce

2/3 cup (5 1/2 oz/165 g) canned soybeans, drained
5 oz (150 g) soft or silken tofu, drained
1/3 cup (3 fl oz/90 ml) lemon juice
1/4 cup (2 oz/60 g) tahini (sesame paste)
2 teaspoons white (shiro) miso
salt and cracked pepper to taste
2 garlic cloves, finely chopped
2 tablespoons finely chopped fresh parsley
1/4 teaspoon cayenne pepper or finely chopped seeded chili pepper

To make sesame crackers: Preheat oven to 350°F (180°C). Line a baking sheet, about 12 x 9 inches (30 x 23 cm), with parchment (baking) paper.

In a large bowl, combine all ingredients and stir well. Spread mixture thinly onto baking sheet and bake until crisp, 10–15 minutes. Cut into pieces while warm or let cool on tray and break into pieces.

In a food processor, puree soybeans until fairly smooth. Add tofu, lemon juice, tahini, miso, salt, pepper and garlic and process until smooth. Stir in parsley, chives and cayenne. Serve with sesame crackers and vegetable sticks.

Serves 6–8

Variation: Serve tahini tofu as a sauce with grilled fish or steak. You can also use it as a filling in wraps, savory pancakes or sandwiches.

Miso and Spinach Scallops

1 cup (1 oz/30 g) packed spinach leaves, washed
1 tablespoon white (shiro) miso
1 tablespoon mirin
1/2 teaspoon sugar
1 tablespoon water
12 sea scallops
slivers of lemon zest for garnish

Preheat oven to 400°F (200°C). Line a baking sheet with parchment (baking) paper.

Blanch spinach in boiling water for 1 minute. Drain. In a food processor, puree spinach. Add miso, mirin, sugar and water. Process until mixture is smooth and sugar is dissolved.

Place scallops on baking sheet and spoon spinach mixture on top of scallops and bake until scallops are just opaque throughout, 3–4 minutes. Be careful not to overcook the scallops or they will become tough. Garnish with lemon zest and serve immediately.

Serves 4

Variations: Scallops can be cooked and served in their shells or in small ramekins.

Substitute oysters or mussels for scallops.

Left: Spicy Tahini Tofu with Sesame Crackers

Fresh Spring Rolls

For dipping sauce

4 oz (125 g) silken tofu, drained and pureed

1/4 cup (2 fl oz/60 ml) sweet chili sauce

2 teaspoons fresh lemon juice

pinch salt (optional)

1 1/2 oz (45 g) dried rice flour (vermicelli) noodles

1 cup (2 oz/60 g) soybean sprouts, blanched

1 medium carrot, julienned

1/2 red bell pepper (capsicum), seeded and julienned

6 snow peas (mange-tout), julienned

1 cup (2 oz/60 g) finely shredded Chinese (napa) cabbage

2 1/2 oz (75 g) extra-firm tofu, drained and shredded

1 tablespoon chopped cilantro (fresh coriander) leaves

1 tablespoon finely chopped fresh mint

24 rice papers, about 6 inches (15 cm) square

To make dipping sauce: In a food processor, puree tofu. Add remaining ingredients and process until smooth.

Put noodles in a large bowl and cover with boiling water. Let stand until noodles are soft, 5–10 minutes. Drain and rinse under cold water. Drain again and pat dry with paper towels.

In a large bowl, combine noodles, soybean sprouts, carrot, bell pepper, snow peas, cabbage, tofu, cilantro and mint. Soak each rice paper separately in warm water until softened, about 30 seconds. Lay each sheet on a dry cloth and pat dry. Put 1 rounded tablespoon of filling on each sheet and roll up tightly, tucking in sides to make parcels. Serve with chili tofu dipping sauce.

Makes 24 rolls

Tofu Salad with Miso Dressing

For miso dressing

2–3 tablespoons white (shiro) miso

1 tablespoon mirin

1 tablespoon sake

1 tablespoon sugar

2 tablespoons rice vinegar or slightly diluted cider vinegar

1 teaspoon soy sauce

1/4 teaspoon hot mustard (optional)

For marinade

2 tablespoons rice vinegar

1 tablespoon sugar

pinch salt

13 oz (400 g) silken firm or fresh tofu, drained and pressed (see page 24)

4 scallions (shallots/spring onions), green parts only, cut into 3/4-inch (2-cm) diagonal slices

wasabi paste or hot mustard

To make dressing: In a small saucepan, combine miso, mirin, sake and sugar and heat until sugar dissolves. Remove from heat and let cool. Stir in vinegar, soy sauce and optional mustard. Refrigerate until required.

In a medium bowl, combine marinade ingredients (or use sushi vinegar). Cut tofu into 3/4-inch (2-cm) cubes and add to marinade bowl. Let stand for 15 minutes. Drain tofu, pat dry and gently mix with dressing. Arrange on plates or in bowls. Garnish with scallions and serve with wasabi or mustard.

Serves 4

Right: Fresh Spring Rolls

Light Meals and Snacks

Tofu Sticks with Chili Cream

For chili cream

2/3 cup (6 oz/180 g) silken tofu, drained
2 tablespoons fresh lemon juice or vinegar
1/4 teaspoon salt
1–2 teaspoons red or white (shiro) miso
1/4 cup (2 fl oz/60 ml) sweet chili sauce

10 oz (300 g) firm tofu, drained and pressed (see page 24)
1/4 cup (1 1/2 oz/45 g) all-purpose (plain) flour for dusting
soybean or canola oil for deep-frying

To make chili cream: In a food processor, puree tofu. Add all remaining ingredients and puree until smooth.

Cut tofu into sticks, about 3/8 inch (1 cm) thick and 1 1/2 inches (4 cm) long. Lightly dust sticks with flour.

Fill a wok or large frying pan one-third full with oil and heat to 365°F (185°C). Deep-fry sticks until golden, 2–3 minutes. Drain on paper towels. Serve immediately, with chili cream.

Serve 4

Variations: Dip tofu sticks into lightly beaten egg and bread crumbs or tempura batter before frying.

Serve tofu sticks and chili cream with fried fish as a main course.

Omit sweet chili sauce and substitute any of the following: minced garlic, curry powder, minced onion or scallion (shallot/spring onion), mustard, Tabasco sauce, tahini, barbecue sauce, cucumber pickles, dried or fresh herbs (parsley, chives, dill, oregano, basil, marjoram), grated fresh ginger, Asian sesame oil or peanut butter.

Spicy Soy and Potato Pastries

2 tablespoons soybean oil
1/4 cup (6 1/2 oz/200 g) pumpkin or butternut squash,
diced into 1/2-inch (12-mm) pieces
1 1/4 cups (6 1/2 oz/200 g) diced potatoes
1 medium yellow (brown) onion, diced
2 oz (60 g) fresh soybean sprouts
2 teaspoons ground cumin
1 teaspoon ground coriander
1 teaspoon red miso
1/4 teaspoon ground turmeric
1/4 teaspoon salt
3 sheets thawed frozen puff pastry, cut into quarters
1 teaspoon cumin seeds
2 tablespoons soy milk
Minted Yogurt Sauce (page 53)

Preheat oven to 400°F (200°C). Line a baking sheet with parchment (baking) paper.

In a large frying pan, heat oil over medium-low heat and cook pumpkin, potato and onion until they begin to soften, about 5 minutes. Add sprouts, cumin, coriander, miso, turmeric and salt and cook until fragrant, about 2 minutes. Remove from heat.

Put about 2 tablespoons of vegetable mixture in center of each quarter sheet of pastry. Lightly brush pastry edges with soy milk and fold all 4 corners to center, gently folding and pinching edges together to seal. Brush tops with soy milk and sprinkle with cumin seeds. Place on baking sheet and bake until lightly browned and cooked through, about 12 minutes. Serve with minted yogurt sauce.

Makes 12

Left: Tofu Sticks with Chili Cream

Tuna and Whole-grain Mustard Pouches with Crisp Greens

For crisp greens

3¹/₂ oz (105 g) snow peas (mange-tout), trimmed
3¹/₂ oz (105 g) thin asparagus, trimmed and cut into 2-inch (5-cm) lengths
¹/₂ cup (2¹/₂ oz/75 g) fresh or frozen soybeans
1 teaspoon mirin
1 teaspoon soy sauce

2 teaspoons soybean oil
¹/₂ cup (2 oz/60 g) onion, finely chopped
³/₄ cup (6 fl oz/180 ml) soy milk
2 tablespoons cornstarch (cornflour)
3¹/₂ oz (105 g) cooked and flaked tuna, or 1 small can (3 oz/90 g), drained
1 teaspoon whole-grain mustard
¹/₂ cup (3 oz/90 g) corn kernels
2 teaspoons finely chopped fresh dill
4 deep-fried tofu pouches or 4 large deep-fried tofu puffs
dill sprigs for garnish

To make crisp greens: Cook vegetables in a covered steamer over boiling water until tender but still crisp, about 3 minutes. Combine mirin and soy sauce and drizzle over vegetables. Set aside.

Preheat oven to 350°F (180°C). Line a baking sheet with parchment (baking) paper.

In a medium saucepan, heat oil over medium heat and sauté onion until soft, 3–4 minutes. In a cup, mix 1 tablespoon soy milk with cornstarch until smooth. Add to saucepan with remaining soy milk, tuna, mustard and corn. Cook until thickened, stirring continuously, about 5 minutes. Fold in chopped dill.

Cut tofu pouches or puffs in half diagonally and make pockets inside with fingers. Fill pouches with tuna mixture and place on prepared pan. Bake until pouches are just crisp, 7–8 minutes. Arrange 2 filled tofu pouches on each plate with green vegetables and serve immediately, garnished with dill sprigs.
Serves 4

Tip: Filled pouches can be closed, or left open with filling exposed.

Sushi Tofu Pouches (Inari-zushi)

2 tablespoons sesame seeds, toasted
¹/₂ small unpeeled English (hothouse) cucumber, seeded and diced
2¹/₂ cups (12 oz/375 g) Sushi Rice (page 45)
8 seasoned tofu pouches
2 tablespoons red or pink pickled ginger
8 scallions (shallots/spring onions), green parts only, blanched

Fold sesame seeds and cucumber into sushi rice. Gently open cut sides of tofu pouches and fill two-thirds full with rice. Close sides of pouches over rice to seal and turn pouches over so flaps are underneath. Tie a piece of blanched scallion around each pouch and gently tie at the top. Serve with pickled ginger.
Makes 8 pouches

Tip: Seasoned tofu pouches and pickled ginger are available at Asian food stores and some supermarkets.

Right: Tuna and Whole-grain Seeded Mustard Pouches

Teriyaki-tempeh Sushi Rolls

16 strips tempeh, $1/4$ inch (6 mm) wide and 4 inches
(10 cm) long
1 tablespoon teriyaki sauce, soy sauce or ketjap manis
2 sheets toasted nori (yaki-nori)
2 cups (10 oz/300 g) Sushi Rice (page 45)
1 teaspoon wasabi paste
1 small English (hothouse) cucumber, quartered lengthwise
and seeded
2 tablespoons soy sauce
1 tablespoon pink pickled ginger
finger bowl filled with water with a splash of vinegar

Marinate tempeh strips in teriyaki sauce for 10–15 minutes. Cut nori sheets in half, parallel with lines marked on rough side of sheets. Lay 1 half-sheet along long side of a bamboo mat, 3 slats from edge. Dip fingers into water, shaking off excess, and gently spread one-fourth of sushi rice over nori, leaving a 1-inch (2.5-cm) strip free on long side farthest from you.

Spread a dab of wasabi across center of rice, then add strips of tempeh and cucumber, making sure they extend to each end. (Do not overfill, or rolls will split.) Pick up edge of mat nearest to you with thumbs and index fingers and hold filling ingredients with your remaining fingers. Roll mat forward tightly to enclose vegetables. Continue rolling forward to complete and seal roll. Repeat with remaining ingredients. Wipe a sharp knife with a damp cloth and cut each roll into 6 pieces, wiping knife after each cut. Serve with pickled ginger.
Makes 24 pieces

Left: Teriyaki-tempeh Sushi Rolls

Sushi Rice

1 cup (7 oz/220 g) short-grain rice
$1^{1}/2$ cups (12 fl oz/375 ml) water

For sushi vinegar
3 tablespoons rice vinegar
$1^{1}/2$ tablespoons sugar
$1/2$ teaspoon salt

In a medium saucepan, combine rice and water. Bring to a boil, reduce heat to very low, cover and simmer until all liquid is absorbed, about 12 minutes. Remove from heat and stand, covered, for 10 minutes to complete.

Meanwhile, make sushi vinegar: In a small bowl, combine ingredients and mix well.

Spread hot rice in a flat nonmetallic bowl, then drizzle with sushi vinegar. Slice through rice with a wooden spoon to distribute vinegar evenly and break up any lumps. Fan rice with a hand-held fan for a few minutes to cool it to room temperature. Cover rice with a damp cloth to keep it from drying out.
Makes about 3 cups (15 oz/450 g)

Tip: Prepared sushi vinegar is available at Asian food stores and some supermarkets.

If cooking more than 1 cup rice, reduce subsequent amount of water to 1 cup water.

Salmon Crepes with Spinach Mayonnaise

For tofu crepes

2 oz (60 g) silken tofu, drained
1 cup (8 fl oz/250 ml) soy milk
1/4 cup (2 fl oz/60 ml) water
1/4 teaspoon salt
3/4 cup (4 oz/125 g) self-rising flour, sifted
1/4 cup (1 1/2 oz/45 g) soy flour
vegetable-oil cooking spray

For spinach mayonnaise

1/2 bunch spinach (about 2 1/2 oz/75 g), stemmed,
blanched and chopped
10 oz (300 g) silken tofu, drained
2 tablespoons fresh lemon juice
2 teaspoons honey
1 tablespoon light soy sauce
2 teaspoons Dijon mustard
1/3 cup (3 fl oz/90 ml) soybean oil
1 tablespoon finely chopped fresh tarragon
salt and cracked black pepper to taste
Soy milk (optional)

8 oz (250 g) soy cream cheese
14 oz (440 g) smoked salmon or canned red salmon, drained
2 teaspoons white (shiro) miso
2 tablespoons fresh lemon juice
2 tablespoons finely chopped fresh parsley
1 tablespoon finely chopped fresh dill
3 scallions (shallots/spring onions), thinly sliced
cracked black pepper to taste

To make tofu crepes: In a food processor, puree tofu until smooth. Add soy milk, water and salt and puree until well combined. With machine running, gradually add flours, stirring until smooth. Heat an 8 or 9-inch (20 or 23-cm) crepe pan or small frying pan over medium heat. Lightly spray with oil and pour in about 1/4 cup (2 oz/60 g) batter to thinly coat bottom of pan. Cook crepes until lightly browned, about 1 minute each side.

To make spinach mayonnaise: In a food processor, combine spinach, tofu, lemon juice, honey, soy sauce and mustard. Puree until smooth. With machine running, gradually pour in oil in a steady stream. Put mixture into a bowl and stir in tarragon, salt and pepper. Add soy milk if a thinner consistency is preferred.

In a medium bowl, beat cream cheese with an electric mixer until smooth. Stir in salmon, miso, lemon juice, herbs, scallions, and pepper until smooth. Spoon 1/4 cup (2 oz/60 g) mixture onto each crepe, roll and stack on serving plate as they are made. Serve with spinach mayonnaise.

Makes about 10 crepes; serves 4 or 5

Tips: Crepes can be made ahead, stacked with a sheet of freezer plastic between each one and frozen in an airtight container or freezer bag. Frozen crepes are best used within 1 month.

Because these crepes are not sweet, they can be used with both sweet and savory fillings.

Right: Salmon Crepes with Spinach Mayonnaise

Smoked Salmon and Green Peppercorn Frittata

3¹/₂ oz (105 g) soy spiral pasta
1 tablespoon soy spread or oil
1 leek, white part only, rinsed and chopped
4 oz (125 g) silken or fresh tofu, drained
3¹/₂ oz (105 g) extra-firm tofu, drained and shredded
3¹/₂ oz (105 g) smoked salmon, chopped
4 eggs, lightly beaten
1 tablespoon capers, chopped (optional)
1 tablespoon finely chopped fresh chives
2 tablespoons finely chopped fresh dill
cracked pepper to taste
2 oz (60 g) soy and herb cheese, shredded

For green peppercorn sauce
6 oz (180 g) silken tofu, drained
1¹/₂ tablespoons fresh lemon juice
¹/₄ teaspoon salt
1 tablespoon green peppercorns

To make sauce: In a food processor, puree tofu, lemon juice and salt. Fold through peppercorns. Add soy milk if required to thin sauce consistency.

Lightly grease an 8-inch (20-cm) round cake pan and line with parchment (baking) paper.

Cook pasta in salted boiling water until just al dente, 8–10 minutes. Drain and rinse under cold water; drain again. In a large frying pan, heat soy spread over medium heat. Add leek and cook, without browning, until soft, about 5 minutes. Remove from heat and let cool. In a food processor, puree silken tofu until smooth.

In a large bowl, combine pasta, leek, silken and firm tofu, salmon, eggs, capers, chives, half of dill and pepper. Spoon mixture into prepared cake pan. Sprinkle with cheese and remaining dill and bake in a medium 350°F

(180°C) oven until set, about 30 minutes. Let stand 5 minutes before turning out. Serve hot or cold with green peppercorn sauce and salad.
Serves 4

Grilled Tofu with Sweet Pork and Minted Mango

13¹/₂ oz (400 g) firm tofu
2 tablespoons soybean oil with ¹/₂ teaspoon Asian sesame oil
2 cloves garlic, finely chopped
2 teaspoons ground coriander
3 tablespoons coarsely chopped peanuts
10 oz (300 g) lean ground (minced) pork
2 tablespoons palm or brown sugar
1 tablespoon fish sauce
2 tablespoons chopped cilantro (fresh coriander) leaves
1 small red chili pepper, seeded and finely chopped
1 mango, peeled, cut from pit and finely chopped
mint leaves for garnish

Cut tofu into ¹/₂-inch (12-mm) slices. In a large frying pan, heat oils over medium heat and fry tofu until golden, about 2 minutes on each side; remove and set aside. Sauté garlic and ground coriander until garlic is lightly browned, about 2 minutes. Do not let garlic burn. Add peanuts and cook for 1 minute. Remove about 1 tablespoon peanuts to reserve for garnish. Add pork and sugar to pan and stir-fry until pork is lightly browned. Stir in fish sauce, cilantro and chili pepper. Remove from heat. Arrange tofu slices on individual plates and top with pork mixture. Serve with chopped mango, mint and reserved peanuts.
Serves 4

Left: Grilled Tofu with Sweet Pork and Minted Mango

Main Dishes

Sesame-crusted Tofu with Celery Root Mash

For marinade

2 garlic cloves, finely chopped
2 teaspoons grated fresh ginger
2 tablespoons Japanese soy sauce
2 tablespoons fresh lime juice
2 teaspoons finely chopped lemongrass

20 oz (600 g) firm tofu, drained and pressed (see page 24)

For soy and celery root mash

½ cup (4 fl oz/125 ml) dry white wine
1 medium yellow (brown) onion, finely chopped
½ cup (125 ml) chicken or vegetable stock
1½ cups (8 oz/250 g) fresh or frozen soybeans
8 oz (250 g) celery root (celeriac), peeled and diced
1 tablespoon finely chopped fresh mint leaves
1 tablespoon fresh lemon juice

1–2 egg whites, lightly beaten
⅓ cup (1 oz/30 g) white sesame seeds
cooking oil spray
1 large red bell pepper (capsicum), seeded and quartered

In a small bowl, combine all marinade ingredients. Cut tofu into strips ³/4 inch (2 cm) wide and 2¹/2 inches (6 cm) long. Place in a large shallow bowl and pour marinade over. Refrigerate for 1 hour, turning occasionally.

To make mash: In a medium saucepan, heat wine over medium heat. Add onion and cook, stirring occasionally, until onion is soft and wine reduced by half. Stir in stock, beans and celery root and bring to a boil.

Reduce heat and simmer, uncovered, until vegetables are soft, 10–15 minutes. Stir in mint and lemon juice. In a food processor, puree until smooth. Set aside and keep warm.

Drain tofu and pat dry with paper towels. Dip tofu in egg whites, draining any excess, and sprinkle with sesame seeds. Spray a large frying pan with oil and cook tofu over medium-low heat until golden on all sides, 1–2 minutes.

Meanwhile, preheat broiler (grill) or oven. Broil (grill) or bake bell pepper until skin blisters. Discard skin and seeds cut pepper into strips. Serve tofu with bell pepper and celery root mash.
Serves 4

Soy Pasta with Miso Pesto

2 cloves garlic, finely chopped
1 cup (1 oz/30 g) firmly packed basil leaves
1 cup (5 oz/150 g) pine nuts, toasted
4 teaspoons white (shiro) miso
½ cup (4 fl oz/125 ml) soybean oil
8 oz (250 g) dried soy spiral pasta

In a food processor, puree garlic, basil, pine nuts and miso until smooth. While machine is running, gradually pour in oil until well combined.

Meanwhile, in a large pot of salted boiling water, cook pasta until al dente, 8–10 minutes. Drain and toss with miso pesto in a large bowl. Spoon pasta into individual bowls and serve.
Serves 4

Right: Sesame-crusted Tofu with Celery Root Mash

Mini Tofu Balls with Minted Yogurt Sauce and Almond Rice

For minted yogurt sauce

6 oz (180 g) silken firm tofu, drained
3/4 cup (6 oz/180 g) plain (natural) yogurt
2 tablespoons fresh lemon juice
3 tablespoons finely chopped fresh mint
1 clove garlic, finely chopped
salt and cracked pepper to taste

For almond rice

1 1/2 cups (11 oz/330 g) long-grain rice
3 cups (24 fl oz/750 ml) water
1 cup (4 oz/125 g) sliced almonds

10 oz (300 g) extra-firm tofu, drained
4 scallions (shallots/spring onions), finely chopped
1 clove garlic, finely chopped
1/4 cup (1/3 oz/10 g) finely chopped fresh parsley
1 cup (2 oz/60 g) soy and linseed bread crumbs
1/3 cup (1 1/2 oz/45 g) dried currants
1 stalk celery, finely chopped
1/3 cup (3 oz/90 g) tahini (sesame paste)
2 tablespoons Japanese soy sauce
1/2 teaspoon ground cumin
1/4 teaspoon ground coriander
1/8 teaspoon chili paste (optional)
1/2 cup (2 oz/60 g) cornflake crumbs
2 tablespoons soybean or vegetable oil

To make sauce: In a food processor, puree tofu, add remaining ingredients and puree until smooth.

To make almond rice: Toast almonds in a dry frying pan over medium heat until golden.

In a large saucepan, combine rice and water and bring to a boil. Reduce heat and simmer, covered, until liquid is absorbed, 12–15 minutes. Remove pan from heat and let stand, covered, for 10 minutes. Stir toasted almonds into cooked rice.

In a food processor, process tofu until it resembles fine bread crumbs. In a large bowl, combine tofu with scallions, garlic, parsley, bread crumbs, currants, celery, tahini, soy sauce, cumin, coriander and chili paste. Mix well. Form into bite-sized balls and roll in cornflake crumbs.

In a large frying pan, heat oil over medium heat and cook tofu balls until cooked through and golden brown, 8–10 minutes. Serve with minted yogurt sauce and almond rice.

Serves 4

Variation: Thread tofu balls on skewers and grill. Alternatively, place on a baking tray lined with parchment (baking) paper and bake in a 350°F (180°C) oven until golden, 8–10 minutes.

Left: Mini Tofu Balls with Minted Yogurt Sauce and Almond Rice

Chicken with Caramelized Orange and Mint Couscous

2 oranges
3 tablespoons mirin or sweet white wine
1 teaspoon soy sauce
2 teaspoons white (shiro) miso
1/8 teaspoon ground cinnamon
4–6 skinless, boneless chicken breast halves
1 tablespoon canola oil

For stuffing

2 1/2 oz (75 g) firm tofu, drained and crumbled
3 scallions (shallots/spring onions), finely sliced
1/2 cup (2 oz/60 g) dried coarse bread crumbs
1 tablespoon chopped fresh parsley
1 tablespoon chopped fresh chives
1/2 cup (2 oz/60 g) roasted ground macadamia nuts
ground pepper to taste

For orange sauce

2 tablespoons chicken stock
1 teaspoon red miso mixed with 1/4 cup (2 fl oz/60 ml)
orange juice
5 oz (150 g) silken firm or soft tofu, drained and pureed
1 teaspoon reserved grated orange zest

For mint couscous

2 cups (16 fl oz/500 ml) chicken stock
2 cups (12 oz/375 g) instant couscous
2 tablespoons finely chopped fresh mint
2 teaspoons soy spread

Preheat oven to 350°F (180°C).

Grate the zest of 1 orange. Peel both oranges and slice thickly. Combine 1 teaspoon orange zest (reserving rest for sauce), mirin, soy sauce, miso and cinnamon. Put chicken in a shallow bowl and pour marinade over. Cover and refrigerate to marinate at least 30 minutes or overnight. Drain chicken, reserving any marinade. In a large bowl, combine all stuffing. Cut lengthwise along one side of each chicken breast, halfway through, to create pockets. Fill pockets with the stuffing mixture and seal the openings with toothpicks.

In a frying pan, heat oil over medium heat and cook chicken until lightly browned, about 2 minutes on each side. Place chicken on prepared pan and bake until opaque throughout, 12–15 minutes. Remove from oven.

Meanwhile, make sauce and couscous: Add stock to frying pan with any remaining marinade and boil for 5 minutes. Add miso mixture to the frying pan with the pureed tofu and orange zest and heat gently without boiling. Set aside and keep warm.

To make couscous: In a medium saucepan, bring stock to a boil. Remove from heat, stir in couscous, cover and let stand until all liquid is absorbed, 5–10 minutes. Stir in mint and soy spread. Set aside and keep warm.

Remove toothpicks from chicken and serve with orange slices, mint couscous and sauce.

Serves 4–6

Tip: Any leftover stuffing can be spread as a topping on chicken before baking.

Right: Chicken with Caramelized Orange and Mint Couscous

Main Dishes

~

Seared Tofu with Mushroom and Rosemary Sauce

20 oz (600 g) firm or fresh tofu, drained
1/4 cup (2 oz/60 g) soy spread
1 clove garlic, finely chopped
3 oz (90 g) each button, swiss brown and oyster mushrooms, halved if large
2 tablespoons chopped fresh rosemary, plus more for garnish
2 tablespoons all-purpose (plain) flour
2/3 cup (5 fl oz/150 ml) chicken stock
2/3 cup (5 fl oz/150 ml) soy milk
1/4 cup (2 fl oz/60 ml) dry sherry
2 teaspoons Dijon mustard
salt and cracked pepper to taste
1 tablespoon soybean oil
1 tablespoon low-salt soy sauce

Wrap tofu in paper towels, place on a cutting board and gently press with the palm of your hand to remove excess liquid. Cut into 1/2-inch (12-mm) slices. In a medium saucepan, melt soy spread over medium heat. Add garlic, mushrooms and 2 tablespoons rosemary and sauté for 2 minutes, stirring occasionally. Stir in flour and cook for 1 minute. Gradually stir in stock, soy milk and sherry. Add mustard, salt and pepper and cook until sauce thickens and mushrooms are tender, about 5 minutes.

Lightly brush tofu slices with oil. In a large frying pan, cook over medium heat until golden, about 2 minutes on each side. Add soy sauce and cook until sauce has evaporated, about 30 seconds on each side, being careful not to burn tofu. Place tofu on serving plates, top with sauce and garnish with rosemary.

Serves 4

Left: Seared Tofu with Mushroom and Rosemary Sauce

Vegetable Curry with Couscous

2 tablespoons soybean oil
5 oz (150 g) firm or fresh tofu, drained and cut into 3/4-inch (2-cm) cubes
1 large yellow (brown) onion, sliced
1 clove garlic, crushed
2/3 cup (5 oz/150 g) tikka curry paste
2 cups (16 fl oz/500 ml) vegetable or chicken stock
about 4 cups (20 oz/600 g) chopped mixed vegetables, such as carrots, cauliflower, broccoli florets, celery, baby eggplants (aubergines), pumpkin or butternut squash
10 oz (300 g) canned soybeans, drained
10 mini deep-fried tofu puffs, halved
1/2 cup (4 oz/125 g) plain (natural) yogurt

For herb couscous
2 cups (16 fl oz/500 ml) vegetable stock or water
2 cups (12 oz/370 g) instant couscous
1 tablespoon each finely chopped fresh parsley and mint
2 teaspoons soybean oil

In a large saucepan, heat 1 tablespoon soybean oil over medium-high heat and sauté tofu until lightly browned, 2–3 minutes. Remove tofu. Reduce heat, add remaining 1 tablespoon oil to pan and cook onion over medium heat until soft, about 2 minutes. Add garlic and curry paste and cook 1 minute, stirring constantly. Add stock, vegetables, soybeans and both types of tofu, cover and bring to a boil. Reduce heat and simmer, stirring occasionally, until vegetables are soft, about 10 minutes. Add yogurt and simmer, without boiling, until heated through. Serve curry with orange and herb couscous.

To make couscous: In a medium saucepan, bring stock to a boil. Remove pan from heat, stir in couscous, cover and let stand until all liquid is absorbed, 5–10 minutes. Stir in herbs and oil.

Serves 4

Tofu Teriyaki with Vine-ripened Tomatoes and Baby Onions

12 bamboo skewers, soaked in water
13 oz (400 g) firm tofu, drained and pressed (page 24)
2/3 cup (5 fl oz/150 ml) soy sauce
2/3 cup (5 fl oz/150 ml) cooking sake or dry white wine
1/2 cup (4 fl oz/125 ml) mirin or sweet rice wine
1 1/2 tablespoons raw sugar
about 6 small scallions (shallots/spring onions)
12 cherry tomatoes or small vine-ripened tomatoes
1 small green bell pepper (capsicum), seeded and cut into bite-sized pieces
1 small yellow bell pepper (capsicum), seeded and cut into bite-sized pieces
1 bunch arugula (rugola/rocket), stemmed

Pat tofu dry with paper towels and cut into 1-inch (2.5-cm) cubes. In a medium bowl, combine soy sauce, sake, mirin and sugar, stirring until sugar dissolves. Pour marinade over tofu and marinate for 1 hour, turning occasionally.

Light a fire in a charcoal grill.

Cut green tops from scallions, then cut tops into 1 1/2-inch (4-cm) pieces. Drain tofu, reserving marinade, and pat dry with paper towels. Thread tofu, white scallion parts, green scallions pieces, tomatoes and bell peppers alternately onto skewers. Brush with marinade and grill, on all sides until tofu is lightly browned, 2–3 minutes each side. Arrange on arugula leaves and serve.
Serves 4–6

Right: Tofu Teriyaki with Vine-ripened Tomatoes and Baby Onions

Vegetable Burger

1 bunch spinach, blanched and chopped
10 oz (300 g) canned soybeans, drained
5 oz (150 g) fresh white goat cheese, crumbled
3/4 cup (1 oz/30 g) packed fresh mint leaves, finely chopped
2 cloves garlic, finely chopped
1 tablespoon ground cumin
1 teaspoon red miso
salt and pepper to taste
5 oz (150 g) extra-firm tofu, shredded
1/4 cup (1 1/2 oz/45 g) finely diced snow peas
1/4 cup (1 1/2 oz/45 g) finely diced green bell pepper (capsicum)
1 egg, lightly beaten
1/2 cup (2 oz/60 g) cornflake crumbs
2 tablespoons soybean oil
8 brown mushrooms
1 cup (6 oz/185 g) cherry tomatoes
3 oz (90 g) mixed baby salad greens

Preheat oven to 400°F (200°C). Line a baking sheet with parchment (baking) paper.

Drain spinach, squeezing gently to remove excess liquid. In a food processor combine soybeans, cheese, mint, garlic, cumin, miso, salt and pepper. Puree until coarsely chopped. In a medium bowl, combine puree, tofu, snow peas, bell pepper and egg. Mix well. Using 3 tablespoons of mixture, shape into patties, about 3 inches (7.5 cm) in diameter and roll in egg, then in cornflake crumbs. In a large frying pan, heat oil over medium heat and fry patties until golden, 3–4 minutes on each sides.

Lightly brush mushrooms with oil. Place mushrooms and tomatoes on prepared pan and roast until soft, 8–10 minutes. Serve patties on mushrooms with tomatoes and salad greens.
Serves 4

Main Dishes

~

Vegetable and Tofu Thai Green Curry

1 tablespoon soybean oil
2–3 tablespoons Thai green curry paste
5 shallots (French shallots) or
1 yellow (brown) onion, chopped
6 cups (20 oz/600 g) pumpkin or butternut squash, peeled and cut into 3/4-inch (2-cm) cubes
5 oz (150 g) firm or fresh tofu, cut into 3/4-inch (2-cm) cubes
3 baby eggplants (aubergines), about 6 oz (180 g) total, diced
2¹/₄ cups (18 fl oz/560 ml) coconut milk
10 small deep-fried tofu puffs
4 fresh kaffir lime leaves, finely sliced
2 cups (10 oz/300 g) fresh or frozen soybeans
3¹/₂ oz (105 g) green beans, cut into 1-inch (2.5-cm) lengths
¹/₃ cup (¹/₂ oz/15 g) shredded fresh basil leaves
1 tablespoon fresh lime juice
1 tablespoon fish sauce
1 teaspoon palm or brown sugar

In a large frying pan, heat oil over medium heat and cook curry paste and shallots until fragrant, about 2 minutes. Add pumpkin, tofu and eggplant and cook, stirring, for 2 minutes. Add coconut milk, deep-fried tofu and lime leaves and simmer for 10 minutes. Add soybeans and green beans and simmer for 5 minutes. Add basil, lime juice, fish sauce and sugar and stir until sugar dissolves. Serve with steamed rice tossed with cilantro (fresh coriander) leaves.

Serves 4

Left: Vegetable and Tofu Thai Green Curry

Tofu and Vegetables in Red Wine

8 oz (250 g) firm tofu, cut into 3/4-inch (2-cm) cubes
¹/₂ cup (4 fl oz/125 ml) red wine
2 medium unpeeled green apples
2 tablespoons soybean oil
1 large red (Spanish) onion, cut into thin wedges
¹/₄ medium red cabbage cored and shredded
2 medium beets (beetroot), peeled and cut into 3/4-inch (2-cm) cubes
3 tablespoons whole-berry cranberry sauce
1 tablespoon Japanese soy sauce
8 small (1 lb/500 g) small new potatoes (chats), cooked

Marinate tofu in ¹/₄ cup (2 fl oz/60 ml) of red wine for 30 minutes, turning occasionally. Drain, reserving wine. Cut apples into wedges about ³/₈ inch (1 cm) thick. In a large frying pan, heat 1 tablespoon oil over medium heat and sauté tofu until lightly browned. Remove and reserve tofu. Add remaining oil to pan and sauté the onion and apple until apple is lightly browned and onion is soft. Remove and reserve onion and apple. Add cabbage and beets to pan and sauté for 3–4 minutes, stirring well. Return tofu, apples and onions to pan with reserved marinade and remaining red wine, cranberry sauce and soy sauce. Reduce heat to medium-low, cover and simmer, for 20 minutes. Remove lid and simmer until liquid has been absorbed and cabbage is caramelized, 10–15 minutes. Halve potatoes lengthwise, spray with cooking spray and grill or panfry until golden. Serve vegetable mixture with potatoes.

Serves 4

Stir-fried Asian Greens with Tempeh

For garlic flakes
canola oil for deep-frying
3 garlic cloves, thinly sliced

8 dried shiitake mushrooms
3 tablespoons soybean oil
5 oz (150 g) tempeh, cut into thin strips
8 oz (250 g) firm tofu, drained and diced
1 medium yellow (brown) onion, cut into thin wedges
1 clove garlic, finely chopped
8 water chestnuts, thinly sliced, or 6 slices lotus root
14 ears fresh baby corn, halved lengthwise
3 small bunches baby bok choy, chopped
1 cup (2 oz/60 g) soybean sprouts, tails trimmed
1/3 cup (3 oz/90 g) ketjap manis with 1 tablespoon light soy
1 small red chili pepper, seeded and finely chopped
fried shallots (French shallots), for garnish, optional

To make garlic flakes: Fill a small frying pan or saucepan one-third full of oil and heat to 350°F (180°C). Cook garlic slices until golden, about 1 minute. Drain on paper towels.

Soak mushrooms in warm water until soft, about 20 minutes. Squeeze out excess water, discard stems and thinly slice tops. In a wok or frying pan, heat 2 tablespoons oil over medium-high heat and stir-fry tempeh and tofu slices until lightly browned, 3–4 minutes. Remove and drain on paper towels. Add remaining oil to pan and stir-fry onion and garlic until onion is soft. Add tempeh, tofu, water chestnuts, baby corn, bok choy and soybean sprouts and stir-fry until bok choy is wilted, about 3 minutes. Stir in ketjap manis and chili and cook for 2 more minutes to blend flavors. Garnish with garlic flakes and shallots and serve with steamed jasmine rice.
Serves 4

Soy and Spinach Dumplings

1/2 cup (2 1/2 oz/75 g) fresh or frozen soybeans
1 bunch spinach (5 oz/150 g), washed,
chopped and blanched
10 oz (300 g) firm tofu, drained
1/2 cup (2 1/2 oz/75 g) drained oil-packed semi-dried tomatoes, finely chopped
1 cup (2 1/2 oz/75 g) fresh soy and linseed bread crumbs
2 tablespoons finely chopped fresh parsley
1/4 cup (1 oz/30 g) grated Parmesan cheese
4 teaspoons fresh lemon juice
1 egg, lightly beaten
1/4 cup (1 1/4 oz/40 g) pine nuts, toasted and coarsely chopped
3 scallions (shallots/spring onions), finely sliced
salt and cracked pepper to taste
Miso Pesto for serving (page 50)

Cook soybeans in boiling water gently for 2 minutes. Drain and rinse under cold water. In a food processor, combine soybeans and all remaining ingredients and puree until coarsely chopped. Shape about 2 tablespoons of mixture into oval balls and place in a steamer basket lined with parchment (baking) paper. Cook in a covered steamer over gently boiling water until cooked through, 8–10 minutes. Serve with miso pesto.
Serves 4–6 (makes about 32)

Right: Stir-fried Asian Greens with Tempeh

Roasted-vegetable Stack with Herbed Rice

$1/3$ cup ($3/4$ oz/20 g) soybean sprouts

1 cup (7 oz/220 g) long-grain rice

$1^1/2$ cups (12 fl oz/375 ml) water

1 tablespoon finely chopped fresh parsley

$1/2$ teaspoon Asian sesame oil

$2^1/2$ tablespoons soybean oil

2 medium zucchini, halved and cut into
$1/4$-inch (6-mm) thin slices

1 baby or small eggplant (aubergine) ($1/2$ lb/250 g), cut
thinly into $1/4$-inch (6-mm) slices lengthwise

1 small sweet potato, peeled, halved and cut thinly into
$1/4$-inch (6-mm) slices lengthwise

1 red bell pepper (capsicum), seeded and quartered

$1/4$ teaspoon salt

10 oz (300 g) tempeh

1 tablespoon ketjap manis

Cook soybean sprouts in boiling water for 2 minutes. Drain and rinse under cold water and chop coarsely. In a medium saucepan, combine rice and water. Bring to a boil, reduce heat, cover and simmer for 12 minutes. Remove from heat, stir in sprouts and parsley, cover and let stand for 10 minutes.

Combine sesame oil with 1 tablespoon of soybean oil and brush over vegetable slices. Heat a large frying pan over medium heat or a grill pan and fry or grill vegetables in batches until soft. Keep all vegetables, except bell pepper, warm in a low oven. In a food processor, puree bell pepper with 1 tablespoon soybean oil and salt until smooth.

Cut tempeh crosswise into 4 pieces, then cut each piece horizontally into 3 slices. Brush slices with ketjap manis. In a frying pan, heat remaining $1/2$ tablespoon oil oil over medium heat and fry tempeh slices until lightly browned, about 1 minute on each side.

To arrange each stack: Put a tempeh slice on a plate. Pack $1/4$ cup (1 oz/30 g) of rice mixture firmly into a small, flat-bottomed mold or coffee cup about 2 inches (5 cm) in diameter. Unmold onto tempeh slice. Place 1 slice each of tempeh, zucchini, sweet potato and eggplant on top. Repeat with another layer of rice, tempeh and vegetable slices. Spoon pureed bell pepper over top, or around base and serve.

Serves 4

Tip: A mixture of rices, such as wild, brown, or jasmine, add color and flavor to this recipe.

Left: Roasted-vegetable Stack with Herbed Rice

Soybean Nachos with Tofu Guacamole

Tofu guacamole

4 oz (125 g) silken tofu, drained
2 teaspoons white (shiro) miso
1 avocado, peeled, pitted and diced
4 teaspoons white vinegar
1 small garlic clove, minced
1¹/₂ tablespoons lemon juice
salt and pepper to taste

2 teaspoons soybean oil
1 medium red (Spanish) onion, finely diced
1 clove garlic, finely chopped
28 oz (875 g) canned chopped tomatoes
3 tablespoons Worcestershire sauce
3 tablespoons tomato paste
1 teaspoon sugar
¹/₂ teaspoon salt
1 green bell pepper (capsicum), seeded and chopped
2 long green chili peppers, seeded and very finely chopped
10 oz (300 g) canned soybeans, drained
2 tablespoons finely chopped fresh oregano
¹/₄ cup (¹/₃ oz/10 g) finely chopped fresh basil
8 oz (250 g) corn chips

In a large saucepan, heat oil over medium heat and sauté onion and garlic until onion is soft, 3–4 minutes. Reduce heat and add tomatoes, Worcestershire, tomato paste, sugar, salt, bell pepper, chili peppers, soybeans and herbs. Simmer, covered, for 10 minutes, adding water if the mixture becomes too dry. Serve over corn chips, with tofu guacamole.

To make guacamole: In a food processor, process tofu until smooth. In a cup, combine 2 tablespoons pureed tofu with miso and stir until smooth. Add miso mixture to food processor with all remaining ingredients and process until well combined, 20–30 seconds.
Serves 4

Pumpkin and Soybean Risotto

1 cup (5 oz/150 g) fresh or frozen soybeans
4 cups (32 fl oz/1 L) vegetable or chicken stock
2 tablespoons soybean oil
1 red (Spanish) onion, halved and thinly sliced
2 cloves garlic, finely chopped
12 oz (375 g) pumpkin or butternut squash, peeled and cut into ³/₄-inch (2-cm) cubes (about 3 cups)
2 cups (14 oz/440 g) Arborio rice
1 cup (8 fl oz/250 ml) dry white wine
cracked pepper to taste
¹/₃ cup (1¹/₂ oz/45 g) freshly grated Parmesan cheese
2 tablespoons chopped fresh chives

Cook soybeans in boiling water for 2 minutes. Drain and set aside. In a medium saucepan, bring stock to a simmer. In a large saucepan, heat oil over medium heat and sauté onion and garlic until onion begins to soften, 2–3 minutes. Add pumpkin and cook for 5 minutes. Add rice, stirring until opaque, 2–3 minutes. Add wine and cook, stirring constantly, until most of liquid has been absorbed. Add simmering stock, ¹/₂ cup (4 fl oz/125 ml) at a time, stirring until each addition of liquid is absorbed, until rice is al dente, 20–25 minutes. Stir in soybeans during the last 5 minutes of cooking. Serve sprinkled with Parmesan and chives.
Serves 4

Right: Pumpkin and Soybean Risotto

Moroccan Baked Vegetables with Preserved Lemon

10 oz (300 g) silken firm or firm tofu, drained
1/3 cup (3 fl oz/90 ml) soybean oil
3 tablespoons fresh lemon juice
6 large tomatoes, cut into wedges
6 garlic cloves, peeled
1 large red (Spanish) onion, peeled and cut into wedges
1 large zucchini, cut into 1/2-inch (12-mm) diagonal slices
1 large red bell pepper (capsicum), seeded and thickly sliced
4 baby Japanese eggplants (aubergines), cut into
1/2-inch (12-mm) diagonal slices
1/4 cup (1/3 oz/10 g) chopped fresh parsley

For sauce
10 oz (300 g) canned soybeans, drained
3/4 cup (6 fl oz/180 ml) vegetable or chicken stock
1 tablespoon tomato paste
1 1/4 teaspoons ground cinnamon
3/4 teaspoon each of ground cumin and ground coriander
1/4 teaspoon each ground turmeric and hot paprika
1 tablespoon rinsed and finely chopped preserved lemon rind

Cut tofu into strips 3/4 inch (2 cm) thick. In a shallow bowl combine 2 tablespoons lemon juice and 3 tablespoons oil. Add tofu and marinate for 20 minutes, turning occasionally. Drain.

Preheat oven to 350°F (180°C) and line a baking sheet with parchment (baking) paper. Put tomatoes and garlic on baking sheet and bake for 35 minutes. Meanwhile, brush onion, zucchini, pepper and eggplant lightly with remaining oil. Put vegetables and tofu on a baking sheet and bake for 20 minutes. In a food processor, combine soybeans, remaining lemon juice, stock, tomato paste and spices and puree until smooth. Pour into a small saucepan, add preserved lemon and heat. Serve vegetables with sauce, garnished with parsley.
Serves 4

Risotto Balls

4 cups (20 oz/600 g) cooled cooked risotto
all-purpose (plain) flour for dusting
canola oil for deep-frying

Shape risotto into bite-sized balls. Dust lightly with flour. Fill a wok or large frying pan one-third full with oil and heat to 350°F (180°C). Fry risotto balls in batches until golden, 2–3 minutes. Drain on paper towels and serve as finger food, or with a green salad for a light meal.
Makes about 24

Tip: This is a good way to use up leftover risotto, but it works just as well with freshly made risotto. If using pumpkin risotto, cut pumpkin into small pieces.

Left: Moroccan Baked Vegetables with Preserved Lemon

Soybean Polenta with Fresh Tomato Sauce

1 tablespoon soybean oil plus extra for brushing
1 medium onion, chopped
1 clove garlic, crushed
4 cups (32 fl oz/1 L) vegetable or chicken stock
1 cup (5 oz/150 g) polenta (cornmeal)
1 cup (5 oz/150 g) fresh or frozen soybeans
2 tablespoons grated Parmesan cheese for serving

For fresh tomato sauce
16 oz (500 g) vine-ripened or plum (Roma) tomatoes, or
13 oz (400 g) canned tomatoes
2 tablespoons soybean oil
1 clove garlic, finely chopped
1 small onion, diced
1 baby Japanese eggplant (aubergine), diced
3 tablespoons tomato paste
2 teaspoons balsamic vinegar
$1/2$ teaspoon sugar
$1/4$ teaspoon salt
2 tablespoons finely chopped fresh parsley
2 tablespoons finely chopped fresh basil
1 tablespoon finely chopped fresh thyme

In a large saucepan, over medium heat, heat 1 tablespoon oil and sauté onion and garlic until onion softens, 3–4 minutes. Add stock and bring to a boil over high heat. Gradually stir in polenta in a steady stream, stirring constantly with a wooden spoon. Reduce heat to medium-low and simmer, stirring occasionally, for 20 minutes. Add soybeans and continue cooking and stirring until polenta is thick and creamy and grains are soft, about 10 minutes. Spread polenta into a lightly greased 9-inch x 12-inch (20-cm x 30-cm) baking dish. Cover and refrigerate until set.

To make sauce: If using fresh tomatoes, bring a saucepan of water to a boil. Cut a small cross in bottom of each tomato and blanch in boiling water for 30–40 seconds. Drain and rinse under cold water. Peel off skin. Halve tomatoes, remove seeds and chop coarsely. In a medium saucepan, heat oil over medium heat and sauté garlic, onion and eggplant until softened but not browned, about 5 minutes. Reduce heat, add remaining ingredients and simmer until tomatoes are soft, 5–8 minutes. Puree in a food processor. Set aside and keep warm.

Cut polenta into 12 pieces and brush with soy oil. In a large frying pan, cook until golden, about 1 minute on each side. Serve with fresh tomato sauce and Parmesan.
Serves 4

Variations: Panfry sliced tofu until golden and serve topped with fresh tomato sauce.

Panfry diced tofu and stir into cooked soy pasta. Toss with fresh tomato sauce.

Tip: For a thinner sauce, add $1/4$ cup (2 fl oz/60 ml) stock, wine or water to sauce mixture.

Right: Soybean Polenta with Fresh Tomato Sauce

Main Dishes

~

Chermoula Soy Pasta with Tofu

For chermoula

2 tablespoons preserved lemon rind, rinsed and chopped

$^1/_3$ cup ($^1/_2$ oz/30 g) packed cilantro (fresh coriander) leaves

$^1/_3$ cup ($^1/_2$ oz/30 g) packed fresh flat-leafed parsley

$^1/_4$ cup (2 fl oz/60 ml) soybean or olive oil

2 tablespoons fresh lemon juice

2 small red chili peppers, seeded and finely chopped

2 cloves garlic, finely chopped

2 teaspoons ground cumin

1 teaspoon sweet paprika

1 teaspoon ground coriander

$^1/_2$ teaspoon salt

20 oz (600 g) firm tofu, drained, pressed (see page 24) and cut into 1-inch (2.5-cm) cubes

8 oz (250 g) dried soy spiral pasta

2 tablespoons soybean oil

5 medium tomatoes, peeled, seeded and diced

2 tablespoons finely chopped fresh parsley for garnish

To make chermoula: In a food processor, combine all chermoula ingredients and process until coarsely pureed.

In a large bowl, combine tofu with half of chermoula, stirring gently so tofu does not break, until well coated. Cover and refrigerate for at least 30 minutes.

In a large pot of salted boiling water, cook pasta until al dente, 8–10 minutes. Drain and toss with remaining chermoula and tomatoes. Place tofu on a lightly oiled grill pan, barbecue or broiler (grill), and broil (grill) until lightly browned, 2–3 minutes on each side. Divide pasta among 4 plates or pasta bowls, sprinkle with parsley and serve topped with tofu cubes.

Serves 4

Baked Potatoes with Herb and Cracked Pepper Cream Cheese

4 unpeeled large russet potatoes, scrubbed

1 clove garlic, finely chopped

4 teaspoons red miso

2 tablespoons soy margarine

2 stalks finely diced celery, finely chopped

$^1/_3$–$^1/_2$ cup (3–4 fl oz/90–125 ml) soy milk

12 cherry tomatoes, halved

vegetable-oil cooking spray

3 oz (90 g) mixed salad greens

For herb and cracked pepper cream cheese

$^1/_2$ cup (4 oz/125 g) soy cream cheese

2 tablespoons each finely chopped fresh sage, thyme and parsley

1 tablespoon lemon juice

2 teaspoons cracked pepper

Steam potatoes until tender, 8–10 minutes. Scoop out and mash potato flesh, reserving jackets. In a cup, combine miso with enough milk to make a smooth paste. Add miso mixture to mashed potato along with margarine, celery and enough milk to make mixture creamy and smooth. Place potato mixture back into reserved jackets. Place jackets on a lightly greased baking sheet with tomatoes, spray with oil and bake in a medium-hot oven (400°F/200°C) until potatoes are golden on top, 10–15 minutes.

To make herb and cracked pepper cream cheese: In a small bowl, combine all ingredients and stir to blend. Serve potatoes with creamed cheese, roasted tomatoes and salad greens.

Serves 4

Left: Chermoula Soy Pasta with Tofu

Seafood

Grilled Swordfish with Creamy Avocado, Lime and Herb Tofu

For creamy avocado, lime and herb tofu

4 oz (125 g) silken tofu, drained

2 teaspoons white (shiro) miso

1 avocado, peeled, pitted and diced

4 teaspoons white vinegar

1 small garlic clove, minced

1¹/₂ tablespoons fresh lime juice

1 teaspoon each finely chopped fresh parsley, chives and mint

salt and pepper

¹/₄ cup (2 fl oz/60 ml) soybean oil

1 clove garlic, crushed

8 slices Turkish or ciabatta bread

4 swordfish steaks or cutlets

1 cup (2 oz/60 g) soybean sprouts, tails removed

1 tablespoon tamari soy sauce

To make creamy avocado, lime and herb tofu: In a food processor, puree tofu until smooth. In a cup, combine 2 tablespoons pureed tofu with miso and stir until smooth. Return to processor with all remaining ingredients and process until well combined, 20–30 seconds. Cover and set aside.

In a small bowl, combine oil and garlic. Lightly brush both sides of bread slices with oil mixture. Preheat an oiled grill pan or frying pan over medium-high heat. Grill bread until lightly browned, 2–3 minutes on each side. Add tamari to remaining oil mixture and brush over swordfish. Cook fish over medium-high heat until lightly browned, 2–3 minutes on each side. Remove.

Panfry soybean sprouts until softened, 1–2 minutes. Serve immediately with Turkish bread and creamy avocado, lime and herb tofu.

Makes 1¹/2 cups (12 fl oz/375 ml); serves 4

Variations: Serve creamy avocado, lime and herb tofu as a dip with sesame crackers (page 37) and vegetable sticks.

Use creamy avocado, lime and herb tofu as a filling for sandwiches, wraps or savory pancakes.

Cut top off baked or steamed whole potatoes and top with creamy avocado, lime and herb tofu mixed with cooked crabmeat.

Add creamy avocado, lime and herb tofu to tacos and enchiladas.

Add wasabi paste or finely chopped chili pepper to creamy avocado, lime and herb tofu for extra bite.

Right: Grilled Swordfish with Creamy Avocado, Lime and Herb Tofu

Seafood

~

Steamed Whole Fish with Miso-tamarind Sauce

2-inch (5-cm) piece tamarind pulp
1/2 cup (4 fl oz/125 ml) hot water
2–3 tablespoons red miso
2 tablespoons palm or brown sugar
2 tablespoons shaoxing wine
2 cloves garlic, finely chopped
1 teaspoon grated fresh ginger
1 stalk lemongrass, white part only, peeled
2 whole snappers (about 1 1/2 lbs/750 g each), cleaned
2 scallions (shallots/spring onions), cut into 1-inch
(2.5-cm) diagonal slices
2 medium red chili peppers, seeded and sliced
2 tablespoons chopped cilantro (fresh coriander) leaves, optional

In a small bowl, combine tamarind and hot water and let stand for 10 minutes. Strain, pressing on solids with back of a spoon. Combine tamarind juice with miso, sugar, wine, garlic and ginger, stirring until smooth. Set aside.

Cut lemongrass into 4-inch (10-cm) lengths. Cut these in half lengthwise and put pieces inside fish. Make 3 diagonal cuts on each side of fish. Lay each fish on a square of parchment (baking) paper. Cover each side of fish with one-half of miso mixture, scatter one-half of scallions and chili peppers over and fold top and bottom of paper over, twisting ends and tucking them under to secure. Refrigerate for 1–2 hours to marinate, turning occasionally.

Cook in a covered steamer over rapidly simmering water until opaque throughout, about 15 minutes. Spoon juices over the fish and sprinkle with cilantro to serve.
Serves 4

Teriyaki and Chili Peaches with Baby Octopus

1 lb (500 g) baby octopus, cleaned
1/4 cup (2 fl oz/60 ml) teriyaki sauce
3 tablespoons mirin
1 tablespoon red miso
1 clove garlic, finely chopped
1 teaspoon packed brown sugar
1 teaspoon grated fresh ginger
1 small red chili pepper, seeded and finely chopped
2 tablespoons soybean oil
1 red (Spanish) onion, cut into thin wedges
2 peaches, peeled, pitted and cut into thick wedges
2 tablespoons finely chopped fresh mint
3 oz (90 g) baby spinach leaves, washed and dried
2 cups (4 oz/125 g) soybean sprouts, blanched

Cut octopus in half if large. In a large bowl, combine teriyaki sauce, mirin, miso, garlic, sugar, ginger and chili pepper. Add octopus and stir until well combined. Cover and refrigerate for 2 hours to marinate. Drain octopus, reserving marinade.

In a large frying pan, heat oil over medium heat and cook onion for 2 minutes. Add peaches and cook for 2 minutes. Remove onion and peaches and keep warm. Add extra oil if needed and cook octopus with marinade in batches until just tender, 3–4 minutes. Combine octopus, onions and peaches with mint and serve over spinach leaves and soybean sprouts.
Serves 4

Left: Steamed Whole Fish with Miso-tamarind Sauce

Grilled Shrimp and Tofu

12 bamboo skewers, soaked in water before use then drained
10 oz (300 g) firm tofu, drained and pressed (see page 24)
24 jumbo shrimp (prawns), shelled and deveined, tails intact
1 clove garlic, finely chopped
2 tablespoons soy sauce
2 teaspoons rice vinegar
1/4 teaspoon Asian sesame oil
1 teaspoon grated fresh ginger
6 scallions (shallots/spring onions), cut into
1-inch (2.5-cm) lengths
ground Szechuan pepper to taste

Light a fire in a charcoal grill.

Cut tofu into 3/4-inch (2-cm) cubes and put in a large shallow bowl with shrimp. In a bowl, combine garlic, soy sauce, vinegar, sesame oil, and ginger and pour over shrimp and tofu. Marinate for 20 minutes, turning occasionally. Drain, reserving marinade. Thread tofu, shrimp and scallions alternately onto skewers. Grill or barbecue, brushing occasionally with marinade, until shrimp are evenly pink, about 3 minutes each side. Sprinkle with Szechuan pepper. Serve with hot cooked noodles such as, udon or hokkien tossed with fresh herbs and lemon juice.

Serves 4–6

Left: Grilled Shrimp and Tofu

Yuba Spring Rolls

2 tablespoons soybean oil
1 medium unpeeled green apple, coarsely shredded
1 medium leek, white part only, rinsed and thinly sliced
3/4 teaspoon ground cumin
3/4 teaspoon ground coriander
3/4 teaspoon ground turmeric
1 teaspoon red miso mixed with 1 teaspoon water
1 medium carrot, grated
1 green bell pepper (capsicum), seeded and thinly sliced
5 oz (150 g) extra-firm tofu, drained and coarsely grated
16 bean curd (yuba) sheets (7 x 8 inches/18 x 20 cm)
salt and pepper to taste
1 egg white, lightly beaten
canola oil for frying
1/4 cup (2 oz/60 g) mango chutney, for serving

In a large frying pan, heat oil over medium heat and cook apple and leeks until leeks are soft, 3–4 minutes. Add cumin, coriander and turmeric and cook for 2 minutes. Remove pan from heat, stir in miso mixture and let cool for a few minutes. Add remaining vegetables and tofu, stirring well to combine.

Dip a yuba sheet in a bowl of warm water to reconstitute, 20–30 seconds. Lay out on a clean cloth or paper towels and pat dry. Spread 2 tablespoons tofu mixture along one side of yuba, leaving about 1 inch (2.5 cm) free at each side. Fold sides of yuba over filling and roll up securely. Brush open edge with egg white to seal.

Fill a wok or large frying pan one-third full with oil and heat to 365°F (185°C). Fry rolls in batches until golden, 2–3 minutes on each side. Serve immediately, with mango chutney.

Serves 4

Vegetables

Green Beans with Lemon Miso

2 tablespoons white (shiro) miso
2 tablespoons mirin or sweet white wine
1/2 teaspoon hot mustard
1/2 teaspoon grated lemon zest
8 oz (250 g) green beans, trimmed and halved
2 scallions (shallots/spring onions), green parts only,
diagonally sliced in 3/4-inch (2-cm) lengths

Mix together miso, mirin, mustard and lemon zest. Bring a medium saucepan of water to a boil, add green beans and simmer until just cooked but still crisp, 3–4 minutes, or microwave on high in a covered container with 1 tablespoon of water for 2–3 minutes. If serving cold, immediately plunge beans into cold water to prevent further cooking. Toss beans with miso mixture and mix well to combine. Serve hot or cold, garnished with scallions.
Serves 4

Baby Eggplants with Miso Plum Paste

4–8 baby eggplants (aubergines), about 16 oz (500 g) total
2 tablespoons soybean oil
1 quantity miso plum paste

For miso plum paste
2 teaspoons white (shiro) miso
4 umeboshi plums pitted, or 3 teaspoons umeboshi paste
1 1/2 tablespoons mirin or sweet white wine

To make paste: In a small bowl, combine miso, umeboshi and mirin and mix until smooth.

Preheat broiler (grill). Cut eggplants in half lengthwise and put on broiling pan (grilling tray). Lightly brush with oil and broil (grill) until just cooked, 2–3 minutes on each side. Spread miso plum paste on cut side of each eggplant half. Return to broiler and broil (grill) until miso starts to bubble, 1–2 minutes. Serve immediately on a bed of mixed salad greens as a light meal or entrée, or as an accompaniment to chargrilled beef or chicken.

Creamy Cauliflower

1–2 slices soy and linseed bread, torn into pieces
1 tablespoon soy spread
1 tablespoon finely chopped fresh parsley
1 tablespoon finely chopped fresh chives
13 oz (400 g) cauliflower, cut into pieces
1 cup (8 oz/250 g) soy cream cheese
1 tablespoon white (shiro) miso

Preheat broiler (grill). Put bread into food processor and process to make about 1 cup (20 oz/60 g) coarse bread crumbs. In a small saucepan, melt soy spread over medium heat, add the bread crumbs, stirring constantly, until the crumbs are crisp. Pour into a bowl and toss with herbs. In a small bowl, mix cream cheese and miso, stirring until smooth. In a covered pot over boiling water, steam cauliflower until just tender but still crisp, 4–5 minutes. Drain and put in a heatproof dish, add cheese and miso mixture. Lightly stir to combine. Sprinkle with bread crumbs and broil (grill) until cheese is hot, 2–3 minutes.
Serves 4

Left: Green Beans with Lemon Miso

Steamed Vegetables with Soy and Ginger

1 yellow (brown) onion, cut into thin wedges
3 baby white bok choy, washed and coarsely chopped
3 baby green (shaughai) bok choy, washed and
coarsely chopped
1 medium fresh jkama (yam bean), peeled and thinly sliced,
or 1 can (7 oz/220 g) water chestnuts, drained
2 tablespoons Japanese soy sauce
1 teaspoon grated fresh ginger
1 cup (2 oz/60 g) fresh soybean sprouts, tails trimmed

In a large frying pan or wok, combine all ingredients, cover and cook over medium-low heat until vegetables are just tender but still crisp, 3–4 minutes, tossing occasionally. Do not overcook. Serve immediately.
Serves 4

Variations: Substitute other Asian greens such as Chinese broccoli (gai lan), Chinese flowering cabbage (choy sum) and/or tat soi for the bok choy. Also, substitute soy sauce with rinsed fermented black soybeans.

Broccoli with Orange and Macadamia Nuts

13 oz (400 g) broccoli, cut into florets
1 tablespoon orange juice
³/₄ teaspoon grated fresh ginger
1 tablespoon soy sauce
1 tablespoon mirin
1 teaspoon grated orange zest
¹/₂ cup (2¹/₂ oz/75 g) macadamia nuts,
toasted and coarsely chopped

In a large frying pan, combine broccoli, orange juice, ginger, soy sauce, mirin and orange zest. Bring to a boil. Reduce heat to medium-low, cover and steam for 3 minutes. Remove lid and cook until broccoli is tender but still crisp, 1–2 minutes. Serve immediately, sprinkled with chopped nuts.
Serves 4

Roasted Garlic, Parsnip and Soybean Mash

3 unpeeled cloves garlic
5 medium parsnips, peeled and chopped
¹/₂ cup (4 fl oz/125 ml) soy milk
1 cup (7 oz/220 g) fresh or frozen soybeans
1–2 tablespoons soy spread
salt and cracked black pepper to taste

Preheat oven to 400°F (200°C). Cook garlic on a baking sheet until soft, about 40 minutes. Alternatively, in a small dry frying pan, cook garlic over medium-low heat for about 15 minutes, shaking pan occasionally to keep garlic from burning. Cook until cloves are soft and skins are lightly browned. When cool, squeeze out flesh and mash with a fork. Steam or cook parsnips in boiling water until soft, 4–5 minutes. Drain. Mash or puree parsnips with garlic and soy milk. Cook soybeans in boiling water until soft, about 2 minutes. Drain. Return parsnip puree to saucepan. Stir in soybeans, soy spread, salt and pepper. Cook until just heated through.
Serves 4

Right: Steamed Vegetables with Soy and Ginger

Vegetables

~

Deep-fried Tofu with Vegetables

13 oz (400 g) firm tofu, drained and pressed (see page 24)
canola oil for deep-frying
3 tablespoons vegetable or chicken broth
3 tablespoons mirin or sweet white wine
2 tablespoons Japanese soy sauce
¹/₄ teaspoon sugar
¹/₂ teaspoon Asian sesame oil
¹/₂ teaspoon grated fresh ginger
1 large carrot, julienned
¹/₂ small green bell pepper (capsicum), seeded and julienned
¹/₂ small red bell pepper (capsicum), seeded and julienned
1 medium red (Spanish) onion, cut into thin wedges
watercress sprigs for garnish

Cut tofu into 1¹/₂-inch (3-cm) cubes and pat dry with paper towels. Fill a large frying pan or wok one-third full with oil and heat to 365°F (185°C). Deep-fry tofu until golden, 3–4 minutes, turning occasionally. Drain on paper towels. In a medium saucepan, combine broth, mirin, soy sauce, sugar, sesame oil and ginger. Bring to a boil, add vegetables and simmer 1 minute. Combine tofu with vegetables and sauce. Garnish with watercress and serve immediately.
Serves 4

Sweet and Sour Tofu

¹/₂ cup (4 fl oz/125 ml) mirin or sweet white wine
¹/₄ cup (2 fl oz/60 ml) Japanese soy sauce
¹/₄ cup (2 oz/60 g) white sugar
¹/₃ cup (3 fl oz/90 ml) rice vinegar
1 lb (500 g) firm tofu, drained and pressed (see page 24)
2 tablespoons soybean oil
1 medium carrot, julienned
1¹/₂ cups (3 oz/90 g) broccoli florets
3 oz (90 g) snow peas, sliced diagonally
3 oz (90 g) green beans, trimmed and cut into
2-inch (5-cm) lengths
1 small red bell pepper (capsicum), seeded and sliced
4 scallions (shallots/spring onions), cut diagonally into
2-inch (5-cm) lengths
1 tablespoon cornstarch (cornflour) mixed with
1¹/₂ tablespoons water

In a small bowl, combine mirin, soy sauce, sugar and vinegar. Stir until sugar dissolves. Dice tofu into ³/₄-inch (2-cm) cubes, place in a large shallow bowl and pour marinade over. Let stand or refrigerate for 15 minutes, turning occasionally. Drain tofu and pat dry, reserving marinade. In a large frying pan, heat half of oil over medium heat and fry tofu until golden brown, 1–2 minutes on each side. Drain on paper towels and keep warm. In same pan, heat the remaining oil and sauté vegetables for 2 minutes, stirring occasionally. Add reserved marinade and cook for 2 minutes. Add some hot liquid to cornstarch mixture, then return to pan and cook, stirring until sauce thickens. Stir in tofu and serve.
Serves 4

Left: Deep-fried Tofu with Vegetables

Salads

Quick-and-easy Soybean Salad

For dressing

¹/₂ cup (4 oz/60 g) white (shiro) miso
3 tablespoons rice vinegar
2 teaspoons tahini (sesame paste)
¹/₄ cup (2 fl oz/60 ml) water

1 teaspoon sugar
1 cup (2 oz/60 g) soybean sprouts
2 cups (14 oz/440 g) canned soybeans, drained
2 stalks celery, finely sliced
6 red radishes, thinly sliced
1 small red bell pepper (capsicum), seeded and thinly sliced
3 scallions (shallots/spring onions), thinly sliced
¹/₄ cup (¹/₃ oz/10 g) finely chopped fresh parsley

To make dressing: Combine all dressing ingredients in a screw-top jar and shake well. Set aside.

Cook soybean sprouts in boiling water for 2 minutes. Drain and rinse under cold water to stop the cooking process. Drain and pat dry with paper towels. Combine with remaining ingredients and drizzle with dressing.
Serves 4

Variation: Fill deep-fried tofu pouches with salad and secure with a toothpick.
Variation for dressing: Combine 1 tablespoon tahini, 3 tablespoons lemon juice and 1 teaspoon miso.

Right: Quick-and-easy Soybean Salad

Thai Red Curry Salad

For dressing

2 tablespoons peanut oil
1 tablespoon fish sauce
1 tablespoon palm sugar
¹/₄ teaspoon Asian sesame oil
1 teaspoon grated lime zest
4 teaspoons fresh lime juice

13 oz (400 g) firm tofu, drained
3 tablespoons Thai red curry paste
2 tablespoons soybean oil
2 cups (4 oz/125 g) soybean sprouts
3¹/₂ oz (105 g) snow peas (mange-tout)
1 small carrot, peeled
2 English (hothouse) cucumbers
2 oz (60 g) baby spinach leaves
1 tablespoon chopped fresh cilantro (coriander)
1 tablespoon finely chopped fresh mint

To make dressing: Combine all dressing ingredients in a screw-top jar and shake well. Set aside.

Cut tofu into ³/₄-inch (2-cm) cubes.

To marinade tofu: In a medium bowl, gently combine tofu, curry paste and oil. Let stand for 30 minutes.

Cook soybean sprouts and snow peas in boiling water for 2 minutes. Drain and rinse under cold water. Drain and pat dry with paper towels. Using a vegetable peeler, slice carrot and cucumber into thin lengthwise strips, discarding cucumber seeds. In a medium frying pan, pan-fry marinated tofu until golden, 2–3 minutes. Arrange sprouts, snow peas, cucumber and carrot strips, spinach and tofu on individual plates. Pour salad dressing over and sprinkle with cilantro and mint.
Serves 4–6

Salads

~

Herb and Lemon Noodle Salad with Ponzu Dressing

For ponzu dressing
$^1/_4$ cup (2 fl oz/60 ml) fresh lemon juice
1 tablespoon soybean oil
1 tablespoon soy sauce
2 teaspoons grated lemon zest
2 scallions (shallots/spring onions), green parts, finely sliced
1 medium red chili pepper, seeded and finely chopped (optional)

1 tablespoon soybean oil
4 oz (125 g) firm tofu, cut into strips $^3/_4$ x 1 inch (2 x 2.5 cm)
1 cup (2 oz/60 g) soybean sprouts
4 oz (125 g) dried soba noodles
1 cup (2 oz/60 g) shredded spinach leaves
1 cup (1$^1/_2$ oz/40 g) finely chopped mixed fresh herbs
such as parsley, chives, oregano, basil
1 cup (6 oz/185 g) finely chopped celery
1 English (hothouse) cucumber, seeded and finely diced, unpeeled

To make dressing: In a small bowl, combine all dressing ingredients and whisk until blended. Set aside.

In a large frying pan, heat oil over medium heat and stir-fry tofu until golden, about 2 minutes each side. Cook soybean sprouts in boiling water for 2 minutes. Using a skimmer, remove sprouts. Rinse under cold water, then drain. Return water to a boil, gradually add noodles and return to a boil. Add $^1/_4$ cup (2 fl oz/60 ml) cold water and bring back to a boil. Add another $^1/_4$ cup cold water, return to a boil and cook noodles until tender, 8–10 minutes total cooking time. Drain noodles, add remaining ingredients and dressing, toss well to combine, and serve.
Serves 4

Fresh Soybean and Fennel Salad

2 tablespoons soybean oil
$^1/_4$ cup finely sliced shallots (French shallots)
1 bunch thin asparagus, trimmed
1 fennel bulb, trimmed and finely sliced
1 cup (7 oz/220 g) fresh or frozen soybeans
$^1/_3$ cup (3 fl oz/90 ml) vegetable or chicken stock
1 tablespoon mirin
2 teaspoons Japanese soy sauce
1 clove garlic, finely chopped
$^1/_8$ teaspoon sugar
salt and white pepper to taste
2 teaspoons each chopped fresh parsley, basil and chives
1 teaspoon mustard seed, walnut or macadamia oil

In a large frying pan, heat oil over medium heat and cook shallots until soft. Add asparagus and fennel and cook until tender but still crisp, 3–4 minutes. Add soybeans, broth, mirin, soy sauce, garlic, sugar, salt and pepper and cook for 2 minutes. Add herbs and toss to combine. Sprinkle with mustard seed oil and serve immediately.
Serves 4

Tip: Serve with poached or grilled fish for a main dish, or toss salad with grilled sliced calamari.

Left: Herb and Lemon Noodle Salad with Ponzu Dressing

Caesar Pasta Salad with Tofu Dressing

For garlic croutons

2 slices soy and linseed bread
2 tablespoons soy spread
1 clove garlic, minced

For dressing

6 oz (180 g) silken or fresh tofu, drained
and pressed (page 24)
3 tablespoons soybean oil
2 tablespoons white vinegar
2 teaspoons Dijon mustard
3 scallions (shallots/spring onions), finely chopped
1 clove garlic, finely chopped
1/4 teaspoon salt
cracked pepper to taste

4 oz (125 g) soy spiral pasta
1 teaspoon soybean oil
1 medium head romaine (cos) lettuce, washed, dried and
torn into pieces
8 anchovy fillets, drained and chopped
4 hard-boiled eggs, quartered
1/2 cup (2 oz/60 g) shaved Parmesan cheese

To make croutons: Preheat oven to 350°F (180°C).

In a small bowl, combine soy spread and garlic. Spread thinly on both sides of bread. Cut bread into 3/4-inch (2-cm) cubes. Spread bread cubes on a baking sheet and bake until crisp and lightly browned, 10–15 minutes. Remove from oven and set aside.

To make dressing: In a food processor, puree tofu until smooth. Add remaining ingredients and puree to combine. Set aside.

In a large pot of salted boiling water, cook pasta until al dente, 8–10 minutes. Drain, rinse under cold water and drain again. In a large bowl, toss pasta with oil. Add lettuce leaves, anchovies, eggs and half of cheese. Drizzle with dressing and toss to combine. Add garlic croutons and serve, sprinkled with remaining Parmesan.
Serves 4

Macadamia and Wild Rice Salad with Lemon and Garlic Dressing

For lemon and garlic dressing
1/2 cup (4 fl oz/125 ml) soybean oil
2 tablespoons fresh lemon juice
1 teaspoon light soy sauce
1 clove garlic, finely chopped
1/4 teaspoon sugar
1/2 teaspoon cracked pepper
pinch salt

1 1/2 cups (9 oz/280 g) soy grits
2/3 cup (3 1/2 oz/105 g) wild rice
4 cups (32 fl oz/1 L) water
1 cup (2 oz/60 g) soybean sprouts
2 medium red bell peppers (capsicums)
5 medium baby yellow squash, 6 1/2 oz (200 g) total, quartered
4 scallions (shallots/spring onions), chopped
1 tablespoon finely chopped fresh parsley
1 tablespoon finely chopped fresh dill
2/3 cup (3 1/2 oz/105 g) macadamia nuts, coarsely chopped

To make dressing: Combine all ingredients in a screw-top jar and shake well. Set aside.

Put soy grits in a heatproof bowl and add boiling water to cover. Let stand for 15 minutes. Drain and pat dry with paper towels.

In a medium saucepan, bring water to a boil and add rice. Return to a boil, reduce heat and simmer gently, uncovered, until rice is tender, about 35 minutes. Drain rice, rinse under cold water and drain again.

Preheat broiler (grill).

Cut bell peppers into quarters, remove seeds and ribs, and broil (grill), skin side up, until the skin blisters and blackens, 5–8 minutes. Put peppers in a paper bag, close bag and let cool to touch. Peel off skin and cut peppers into strips.

Bring a medium saucepan of water to a boil. Add squash and soybean sprouts and simmer, uncovered, until just cooked, 2–3 minutes. Drain, rinse under cold water to stop the cooking and drain again.

In a large bowl, combine soy grits, rice, soybean sprouts, peppers, squash, scallions, herbs and nuts, reserving a few nuts for garnish. Drizzle lemon and garlic dressing over salad and serve.

Variations: Add shredded smoked chicken or grilled calamari for a more substantial dish.

Use the salad mixture as a filling for wraps or sandwiches.

Desserts

Raspberry Mousse

6¹/2 oz (200 g) fresh or frozen raspberries
6¹/2 oz (200 g) silken firm, firm or fresh tofu, drained
6¹/2 fl oz (200 ml) soy milk
¹/4 cup (60 g) sugar
3 teaspoons lemon juice
2 teaspoons gelatin powder or 1 envelope plain gelatin
3¹/2 oz (100 g) fresh or thawed frozen raspberries or
blueberries to decorate
1–2 tablespoons confectioners' (icing) sugar, sifted (optional)

In a food processor, combine raspberries and tofu and puree until smooth. Pour puree into a medium bowl and set aside. In a small saucepan over medium-low heat, combine milk, sugar and gelatin and heat until gelatin dissolves, stirring constantly. Remove from heat and allow to cool for 5 minutes. Add gelatin mixture and lemon juice to raspberry mixture, stirring until well combined. Pour mixture into four lightly oiled ramekins (²/3 cup/5 fl oz/150 ml capacity) or decorative glasses and refrigerate until set, about 1 hour. Decorate with raspberries dusted with sugar to serve.
Serves 4

Variation: Substitute 3 tablespoons soy milk with port.

Fruit Wontons

Wrap a slice of a fresh fruit such as apple, pear, or pineapple, in a reconstituted bean curd sheet (see page 25) or small spring roll wrapper. Seal with egg white and deep-fry in canola oil heated to 365°F (185°C), until golden, about 2 minutes.

Serve immediately, with pureed flavored tofu (try coconut or almond), or flavored soy yogurt, or simply sprinkle with confectioners' (icing) sugar.

Miso Figs with Tofu Cream

8 fresh figs, chilled
2 teaspoons white miso
4 umeboshi plums pitted or 3 teaspoons umeboshi paste
1¹/2 tablespoons mirin or sweet white wine

For tofu cream
6¹/2 oz (200 g) silken tofu, drained
2 tablespoons maple syrup
1 teaspoon vanilla extract (essence)
1 tablespoon fresh lemon juice
pinch salt

In a small bowl, combine miso, umeboshi plums and mirin; stir to blend until smooth. Cut figs in half lengthwise and spread miso mixture on each fig half. Place figs on a small baking sheet and broil (grill) until miso mixture bubbles. Arrange 4 fig halves on each plate with tofu cream and serve immediately.

To make tofu cream: In a food processor, combine all tofu cream ingredients and puree until smooth. Set aside.
Serves 4

Tip: Figs should be well chilled for this recipe so they will contrast with the hot topping.

Left: Raspberry Mousse

Banana and Sweet Ginger Cake

1/2 cup (4 oz/125 g) soy butter at room temperature
1 cup (8 oz/250 g) sugar
1 teaspoon vanilla extract (essence)
2 eggs
2 medium bananas, mashed
1/3 cup (2 oz/60 g) finely chopped glacé ginger
1 cup (5 oz/150 g) self-rising flour
1/2 cup (2 1/2 oz/75 g) soy flour
1 teaspoon baking powder
1 teaspoon ground cinnamon
1/4 cup (2 fl oz/60 ml) soy milk
1/4 cup (1 1/2 oz/45 g) soy grits, soaked and roasted, or
chopped roasted nuts

For lemon and cream cheese frosting

4 oz (125 g) soy cream cheese
1 teaspoon honey
1 teaspoon fresh lemon juice
3 tablespoons confectioners' (icing) sugar, sifted
1 teaspoon grated lemon zest

Preheat oven to 325°F (170°C). Lightly grease a 7-inch (18-cm) round cake pan and line the bottom with parchment (baking) paper.

In a large bowl, beat butter, sugar and vanilla until light and fluffy. Beat in eggs, one at a time. Stir in banana, then ginger. Sift flours, baking powder and cinnamon together in a bowl and stir half into cake mixture. Stir in soy milk and remaining flour. Pour batter into prepared pan and bake until a skewer inserted in center of cake comes out clean, about 1 hour. Remove from oven and let cool completely in pan.

To make frosting: Combine all frosting ingredients in a small bowl and beat until smooth.

Spread top and sides of cake with frosting. Sprinkle with roasted soy grits.

Note: To soak and roast soy grits: Soak soy grits in water for 15 minutes. Drain and pat dry. Spread grits on a baking sheet and roast in preheated 350°F (180°C) oven until golden, about 10 minutes. These can be prepared ahead and stored in an airtight container for 1 week.

Miso Baked Pears

4 medium pears, skin on
1/4 cup (1 oz/30 g) chopped pecans
1 cup (6 oz/185 g) finely chopped dates, loosely packed
4 level teaspoons white miso
1 teaspoon firmly packed brown sugar
1/4 teaspoon grated lemon rind
pinch Chinese five spice powder
cooking oil spray

Core pears reserving tops for use as lids. In a small bowl, combine pecans, dates, miso, sugar and lemon rind and five spice powder. Fill cored pears with mixture and cover with reserved tops. Spray a baking dish with cooking oil spray or line it with baking paper. Place pears in dish upright and bake, uncovered, in a moderate oven (350°F/180°C) until cooked but still crisp, 20–25 minutes. Serve warm or chilled, with vanilla bean custard (see page 99).

Right: Banana and Sweet Ginger Cake

Lemon Cream Tarts

For pastry

1/2 cup (1 1/2 oz/45 g) rolled oats
3/4 cup (4 oz/125 g) all-purpose (plain) flour, sifted plus extra for rolling
1/4 cup (1 oz/30 g) soy flour
1/4 cup (1 oz/30 g) flaked (desiccated) coconut
1 teaspoon ground cinnamon
1/4 teaspoon salt
1/4 cup (2 fl oz/60 ml) soybean oil
2 oz (60 g) silken firm or fresh tofu, drained and pureed
2 tablespoons water

For filling

12 oz (375 g) silken firm or fresh tofu, drained
4 teaspoons grated lemon zest
2 teaspoons Japanese light soy sauce
1/4 cup (2 oz/60 g) sugar
1/2 cup (4 fl oz/125 ml) fresh lemon juice
3 teaspoons gelatin powder or 1 1/2 envelopes plain gelatin
3 oz (90 g) soy or dark chocolate

To make pastry: Preheat oven to 350°F (180°C). In a large bowl, combine oats, both flours, coconut, cinnamon and salt. In a small bowl, combine oil, tofu and water. Stir tofu into flour mixture to make a dough, adding extra water if mixture is too dry. On a lightly floured work surface, roll out dough about 1/8 inch (3 mm) thick. Cut dough into 4-inch (10-cm) rounds and gently fit rounds into non-stick or lightly oiled muffin cups or individual tart pans. Bake for 15 minutes.

Remove from oven and let cool (pastry can be prepared ahead and stored in an airtight container for no longer than 5 days).

To make filling: In a food processor, combine tofu, lemon zest and soy sauce and puree until smooth. In a small saucepan, combine lemon juice, sugar and gelatin and stir over low heat until sugar and gelatin dissolve. Cool mixture for 5 minutes. Combine gelatin mixture with the tofu mixture, pour into pastry cups and refrigerate until set, about 30 minutes.

In a double boiler, over barely simmering water or in a microwave on medium heat, melt chocolate. Drizzle chocolate over lemon tarts in a decorative pattern and serve.

Makes 12 tarts

Quick-and-easy Fruit Cream

10 oz (300 g) frozen blueberries, raspberries or strawberries
10 oz (300 g) silken tofu, drained
1–2 tablespoons maple syrup
sliced fresh fruit or berries for serving

Let fruit stand at room temperature for 10 minutes. In a food processor, combine fruit, tofu and maple syrup. Puree until smooth. Pour into decorative glasses, bowls or decorative cups and serve immediately with fresh fruit or thin wafer biscuits.

Serves 4

Variation: Alternate layers of chilled cream with fresh fruit or slices of sponge cake in tall glasses.

Left: Lemon Cream Tarts

Apple and Ginger Puddings

³/₄ cup (6 fl oz/180 ml) soy milk
1³/₄ cups (13 oz/400 g) packed brown sugar
2 eggs, lightly beaten
1¹/₂ cups (7¹/₂ oz/235 g) all-purpose (plain) flour
¹/₄ cup (1 oz/30 g) soy flour
1 teaspoon baking soda
2 teaspoons ground cinnamon
1 teaspoon ground ginger
³/₄ teaspoon salt
¹/₂ cup (3 oz/90 g) finely chopped glacé ginger
3 apples, unpeeled, cored and grated

Preheat oven to 350°F (180°C). In a large bowl, combine soy milk, brown sugar and eggs. Stir until smooth. Sift flours, baking soda, spices and salt together into a medium bowl. Stir dry ingredients into milk mixture. Stir in ginger and apple. Spoon mixture into 8 large teacups or 1-cup (8-fl oz/250-ml) soufflé dishes. Put cups into a baking dish and add enough water to baking dish to come halfway up sides of cups. Bake for 30 minutes. Remove cups from water and return to oven on a baking sheet for 15–20 minutes until a skewer inserted in center of pudding comes out clean. Served hot or chilled, with vanilla bean custard (page 99).

Variation: Cover cups with plastic wrap and cook in a covered steamer over gently boiling water for 45–50 minutes.
Makes 8

Coconut-mango Ice Cream

1 cup (8 fl oz/250 ml) water
1 cup (8 oz/250 g) sugar
10 oz (300 g) coconut-flavored tofu, drained
1¹/₄ cups (8 oz/250 g) mango, diced
1 tablespoon shredded coconut, toasted (see note)
1 tablespoon sliced almonds, toasted (see note)

In a medium saucepan, combine water and sugar and bring to a boil, stirring until sugar has dissolved. Continue boiling gently for 7 minutes. Remove from heat and let cool to room temperature.

In a food processor, puree tofu and mango until smooth. With machine running, gradually pour in syrup and process until combined. Pour into an airtight container and freeze for 2 hours. Remove from freezer and whisk mixture with a fork. Freeze for 2 hours more. Whisk again and return to freezer until frozen. Cut ice cream into slices and sprinkle with coconut and almonds to serve.
Serves 4–6

Note: To toast almonds and coconut: Toast in separate dry frying pans over medium heat until lightly browned, stirring constantly.

Variation: Use a melon baller or small ice cream scoop to shape balls of ice cream and serve them in waffle or chocolate cups, sprinkled with grated soy chocolate. Waffle cups and chocolate cups are available at most supermarkets.

Caramelized Apple and Tofu Pancakes with Cinnamon Cream Cheese

4 unpeeled medium Granny Smith apples, cored
1/4 cup (2 oz/60 g) soy margarine
1/4 cup (3 oz/90 ml) honey
1/2 teaspoon ground cinnamon

Tofu pancakes

2 oz (60 g) silken tofu, drained and pureed
1 cup (8 fl oz/250 ml) soy milk
1/4 cup (2 fl oz/60 ml) water
3/4 cup (4 oz/125 g) self-rising flour
1/4 cup (1 oz/30 g) soy flour
1/4 teaspoon salt
vegetable-oil cooking spray

Cinnamon cream cheese

4 oz (125 g) soy cream cheese
1 teaspoon fresh lemon juice
1/4 teaspoon ground cinnamon
4 teaspoons confectioners' (icing) sugar, sifted
1 teaspoon white (shiro) miso

To make cinnamon cream cheese: Combine all cinnamon cream cheese ingredients in a small bowl, stirring until smooth.

Cut apples horizontally into slices 1/4 inch (6 mm) thin. In a large frying pan, melt margarine over medium low heat. Add honey, cinnamon and apple slices and cook until apple is softened and caramelized, 10–15 minutes, turning slices occasionally.

To make pancakes: In a large bowl, combine pureed tofu, milk and water. In a small bowl, stir flours and salt together. Stir into milk mixture until smooth. Spray a large frying pan with oil, heat over medium heat. For each pancake pour about 2 tablespoons batter into pan and cook, turning, until golden, about 2 minutes each side. Keep warm in a low oven while cooking remaining batter. Arrange alternate layers of apples and pancakes on each plate and serve with cinnamon cream cheese.
Serves 4

Variation: Omit cream cheese and serve pancakes with vanilla soy yogurt or Vanilla Bean Custard.

Vanilla Bean Custard

1 1/4 cups (10 fl oz/300 ml) whole soy milk
1 vanilla bean, halved lengthwise and scraped
2 teaspoons cornstarch (cornflour)
1/4 teaspoon grated nutmeg
1 tablespoon packed brown sugar
1 teaspoon vanilla extract (essence)

In a medium saucepan, combine all ingredients and stir over medium heat until thickened, about 5 minutes. Remove vanilla pod before serving. Serve with Apple and Ginger Pudding (page 98) with fresh fruit or crepes.

Soy Drinks

Banana and Passion Fruit Smoothie

2 small ripe bananas, chopped
2 cups (16 fl oz/500 ml) soy milk
4 teaspoons honey
2 teaspoons vanilla essence
pulp of 2 passion fruits
1/4 teaspoon ground cinnamon

In a food processor or blender, combine bananas, soy milk, honey and vanilla. Stir in passion fruits and serve, sprinkled with cinnamon.
Makes about 2 1/2 cups (20 fl oz/625 ml)

Cantaloupe and Pineapple Smoothie

1 1/3 cups (8 oz/250 g) chopped cantaloupe (rockmelon)
1 cup (8 fl oz/250 ml) low-fat soy milk
1 tablespoon maple syrup
1/2 cup (3 oz/90 g) chopped fresh pineapple
1 teaspoon fresh lemon juice
1 teaspoon chopped fresh mint or mint sprigs for garnish

In a food processor, combine cantaloupe and pineapple. Puree for 2 minutes. Add soy milk and maple syrup and continue processing until smooth. Serve, garnished with mint.
Makes 2 1/2 cups (20 fl oz/625 ml)

Right: Banana and Passion Fruit Smoothie

Soy Drinks

~

Chilled Chocolate

1 tablespoon unsweetened cocoa powder
1 cup (8 fl oz/250 ml) soy milk
¼ cup (2 oz/60 6) vanilla soy yogurt
1 teaspoon honey or sugar to taste
1 teaspoon soy germ powder

In a glass, combine cocoa with a little soy milk and whisk until cocoa dissolves. Stir in remaining soy milk and remaining ingredients and serve chilled.
Makes 1¹/3 cups (11 fl oz/340 ml)

Variation: Add ¹/3 cup (2 fl oz/60 ml) strong cold percolated or 1 teaspoon instant coffee powder for a mocha-flavored drink.

Hot Marshmallow Mocha

1 tablespoon unsweetened cocoa powder
1 teaspoon soy flour
1 cup (8 fl oz/250 ml) soy milk
1 teaspoon instant coffee granules or ¼ cup (2 fl oz/60 ml)
cold strong coffee
1¹/2 teaspoons honey
2 white marshmallows
pinch ground cinnamon or extra cocoa powder

In a cup, combine cocoa and flour with 2 tablespoons of milk and stir to a paste. In a small saucepan over medium heat, combine remaining milk, coffee and honey. Stir in cocoa mixture and simmer for 2–3 minutes, stirring occasionally.

Do not allow to boil. Pour into a mug and top with two white marshmallows and a sprinkling of cinnamon.
Makes about 1 cup (8 fl oz/250 ml)

Spicy Tomato

about 3¹/2 cups (28 fl oz/850 ml) tomato juice
3 tablespoons fresh lemon juice
1 tablespoon teriyaki sauce
a few drops Tabasco
strips of lemon zest (made with a lemon zester)
mint sprigs for garnish

In a glass, combine tomato juice, lemon juice, teriyaki sauce and Tabasco sauce. Stir well and serve chilled, garnished with lemon zest and a mint sprig.
Makes 3²/3 cups (29 fl oz/900 ml)

Left: Chilled Chocolate

103

Berry Smoothie

2 cups (8 oz/250 g) strawberries, hulled, and/or raspberries
6¹/2 oz (200 g) berry soy yogurt
¹/2 cup (4 fl oz/125 ml) soy milk
2 teaspoons honey

In a food processor or blender, puree or blend all
ingredients until smooth.
Makes 2 cups (16 fl oz/500 ml)

Variation: Substitute or add fresh or thawed frozen
blueberries.

Honeyed Strawberry Shake

6¹/2 oz (200 g) silken tofu, drained
2 cups (8 oz/250 g) fresh strawberries, washed and hulled
2 medium bananas, chopped
1¹/2 cups (12 fl oz/375 ml) soy milk
2 teaspoons honey

In a food processor, combine tofu, strawberries and
banana and puree for 2 minutes. Add soy milk and honey
and continue processing until smooth.
Makes about 2¹/2 cups (20 fl oz/625 ml)

Fruity Soy Popsicles (Iceblocks)

1 cup (7¹/2 oz/ 235 g) pureed fruit such as, pineapple,
peaches, strawberries, or bananas
¹/2 cup (4 fl oz/125 ml) soy milk
1 tablespoon honey or maple syrup

Combine pureed fruit, soy milk and honey, mixing until
smooth. Freeze in popsicle (iceblock) molds for at least 2
hours, inserting wooden sticks after mixture has partially
frozen.
Makes 6 popsicles

Variation: For extra creaminess, add ¹/4 cup (2 oz/60 g)
plain (natural) or flavored soy yogurt to mixture.

Tip: Most of soy smoothies and soy drinks can be frozen,
sit at room temperature for a few minutes before serving
as popsicles or desserts.

Right: Berry Smoothie

Glossary

Chili peppers: As a general rule, the smaller the chili pepper the hotter it is. For a milder taste, remove the seeds and membrane of chili pepper before adding to dishes. Dried chili pepper flakes and chili powder can be substituted.

Chinese (napa) cabbage: Milder in flavor than regular cabbage. Cook for a minimum of time to retain crunchy texture or use whole leaves to wrap food.

Chinese five-spice powder: This is made of an equal mixture of ground Szechuan peppercorns, star anise, fennel, cloves and cinnamon. Available at most supermarkets.

Coconut milk and cream: These are made from grated coconut flesh (not the liquid inside coconuts). Thicker coconut cream adds more flavor than the thinner coconut milk. Available in cans from supermarkets.

CURRIES

Massaman curry paste: A mild curry paste with a hint of cinnamon, nutmeg and cloves. Not as hot as Thai green or red curry paste.

Thai green curry paste: A hot curry paste. Thai red curry paste can be substituted.

Tikka masala curry paste: A mild curry paste. Other curry pastes can be substituted.

Dashi: Japanese fish broth made from dried bonito fish flakes (katsuobushi) and konbu/kombu (a seaweed). Available in concentrated liquid, powder or dried granules from Asian food stores. Combine with water to the required consistency. Substitute other stocks.

Fish sauce: Also known as nam pla, nuoc nam and patis, this distinctive, salty sauce is made from fermented shrimp or fish and is used similarly to soy sauce to enhance and balance the flavor of dishes. Some are much saltier than others; use sparingly and add to taste.

GINGER

Glacé (cooking) ginger: Diced fresh ginger cooked in a sugar syrup. Available from supermarkets.

Pink pickled ginger and red pickled ginger: Fresh ginger thinly sliced or shredded and pickled in sweet vinegar. Red ginger (gari) is slightly saltier than pink (beni shoga). Traditionally accompanies sushi and sashimi. Available in jars and packets from Asian food stores and some supermarkets.

Jicama (yam bean): Also known as sweet turnip. Has crunchy and slightly sweet flesh. Peel before use in stir-fries. Available fresh from Asian food stores. Water chestnuts can be substituted.

Kaffir lime: The distinctive fragrant double leaves and fruit of this Asian tree are increasingly available fresh from Asian and many Western supermarkets. Frozen and dried leaves and frozen fruit are also available but lack the flavor of the fresh.

Lemongrass: A popular lemon-scented grass used in Asian-style dishes. Use only the white part or the bulb. Trim the root and remove the outer layer. Chop finely or bruise by hitting with a meat mallet or blunt side of a chef's knife to bring out the flavor.

Lotus root: A root vegetable that can be stuffed or sliced and added to stir-fries for a crunchy texture. Available frozen, canned and sometimes fresh from Asian food stores. Scrape fresh lotus root and soak in water with a dash of vinegar or lemon juice to stop discoloration. Water chestnuts or jicama (yam bean) can be substituted.

Mirin: A sweet Japanese rice wine used for cooking. Sweet sherry can be substituted.

Palm sugar: The sap of the palm tree, reduced to a moist sugar. Popular in Asian cuisine. The darker the color the more caramel the flavor. Brown sugar can be substituted. Available in wrapped blocks or jars. Thinly shave sugar off blocks with a knife or vegetable peeler. Keep the lid on jars tightly or the sugar can dry out.

Preserved lemons: Lemons preserved in mixture of salt and lemon juice and sometimes spices for about a month. Distinctive flavor popular in Moroccan cooking. Pulp can be used but is usually discarded and only the rind is used.

Rice paper wrappers: Flavorless, edible, transparent wrappers used to wrap food to be eaten as is or deep-fried. Available square or round and in large and small sizes in Asian food stores and some supermarkets.

Rice vinegar: A mild vinegar made from rice. Used to make sushi vinegar. Substitute distilled cider vinegar, but dilute with a little water as flavor is too strong.

Sake: A dry Japanese rice wine used for cooking. Not the same as sake for drinking. Dry sherry or Chinese cooking wine can be substituted.

Shaoxing wine: Chinese rice wine for cooking. Dry or sweet sherry, mirin (sweet rice wine) or cooking sake (dry rice wine) can be substituted.

Shichimi (Seven spices): Also known as shichimi togarashi and seven-spice seasoning, this peppery Japanese condiment is made up of seven different seasonings: red chili pepper flakes (togarashi), white sesame seeds, nori (seaweed) flakes, sansho (Japanese prickly ash berries), white poppy seeds, black hemp seeds and dried mandarin orange peel. Available in small jars from Asian food stores.

Shiitake mushrooms: Also known as Chinese black mushrooms. Available fresh and dried from supermarkets and Asian food stores. Dried shiitake, which have a much stronger flavor than fresh, should be soaked in warm water for 20 minutes to soften. Stem both fresh and dried shiitake before use.

Sweet chili sauce: Use as a dipping sauce or combine with other sauces, such as soy, plum or ketjap manis. May also contain garlic and/or ginger. Hotter and less-sweet chili sauces may be substituted.

Tahini (sesame paste): A smooth paste made from ground sesame seeds. Some are thicker than others, so add extra water if required. Available from most supermarkets.

Tamarind pulp: Available as powder, paste or pulp, this popular Asian fruit adds a sour flavor. Soak pulp required in hot water for about 15 minutes, then push through a fine-mesh sieve to extract the liquid, discarding the pulp. Dissolve powders and pastes before use, but be aware that some can be quite salty.

Umeboshi: Pickled Japanese plums with a tart, salty flavor. Available whole or pureed (umeboshi paste) in Asian food stores.

Vermicelli noodles: Very thin noodles made of rice flour. Sometimes referred to as cellophane noodles. Available dried in Asian food stores and supermarkets.

Wasabi: Very hot, Japanese green horseradish, traditionally served with sushi and sashimi. Available ready to use in tubes, powder that is mixed with water but only as required as pungency is easily lost. Occasionally available fresh; peel and finely grate in a circular motion.

Index

Guide to Weights and Measures

WEIGHTS

Imperial	Metric
$^1/_3$ oz	10 g
$^1/_2$ oz	15 g
$^3/_4$ oz	20 g
1 oz	30 g
2 oz	60 g
3 oz	90 g
4 oz ($^1/_4$ lb)	125 g
5 oz ($^1/_3$ lb)	150 g
6 oz	180 g
7 oz	220 g
8 oz ($^1/_2$ lb)	250 g
9 oz	280 g
10 oz	300 g
11 oz	330 g
12 oz ($^3/_4$ lb)	375 g
16 oz (1 lb)	500 g
2 lb	1 kg
3 lb	1.5 kg
4 lb	2 kg

VOLUME

Imperial	Metric	Cup
1 fl oz	30 ml	
2 fl oz	60 ml	$^1/_4$
3 fl oz	90 ml	$^1/_3$
4 fl oz	125 ml	$^1/_2$
5 fl oz	150 ml	$^2/_3$
6 fl oz	180 ml	$^3/_4$
8 fl oz	250 ml	1
10 fl oz	300 ml	$1^1/_4$
12 fl oz	375 ml	$1^1/_2$
13 fl oz	400 ml	$1^2/_3$
14 fl oz	440 ml	$1^3/_4$
16 fl oz	500 ml	2
24 fl oz	750 ml	3
32	1L	4

USEFUL CONVERSIONS

$^1/_4$ teaspoon		1.25 ml
$^1/_2$ teaspoon		2.5 ml
1 teaspoon	5 ml	
1 Australian tablespoon	20 ml (4 teaspoons)	
1 UK/US tablespoon	15 ml (3 teaspoons)	

Butter/Shortening

1 tablespoon	$^1/_2$ oz	15 g
$1^1/_2$ tablespoons	$^3/_4$ oz	20 g
2 tablespoons	1 oz	30 g
3 tablespoons	$1^1/_2$ oz	45 g

OVEN TEMPERATURE GUIDE

The Celsius ($^\circ$C) and Fahrenheit ($^\circ$F) temperatures in this chart apply to most electric ovens. Decrease by 25°F or 10°C for a gas oven or refer to the manufacturer's temperature guide. For temperatures below 325°F (160°C), do not decrease the given temperature.

Oven description	$^\circ$C	$^\circ$F	Gas Mark
Cool	110	225	$^1/_4$
	130	250	$^1/_2$
Very slow	140	275	1
	150	300	2
Slow	170	325	3
Moderate	180	350	4
	190	375	5
Moderately Hot	200	400	6
Fairly Hot	220	425	7
Hot	230	450	8
Very Hot	240	475	9
Extremely Hot	250	500	10

First published in the United States in 2002 by Periplus Editions (HK) Ltd.,
with editorial offices at 153 Milk Street, Boston, Massachusetts 02109 and
130 Joo Seng Road #06-01/03
Olivine Building, Singapore 368357

Commissioned by Deborah Nixon
Text: Brigid Treloar
Nutritionist: Karen Inge
Photographer and Stylist: Vicki Liley
Home Economist: Christine Chandler
Designer: Robyn Latimer
Editors: Merry Morgan Pearson and Carolyn Miller
Production Manager: Sally Stokes
Project Coordinator: Alexandra Nahlous

Library of Congress Cataloging-in-Publication Data is available.
ISBN 0-7946-5010-4

DISCLAIMER
This book is intended to give general information only
and is not a substitute for professional and medical advice.

DISTRIBUTED BY

North America	Japan and Korea	Asia Pacific
Tuttle Publishing	Tuttle Publishing	Berkeley Books Pte. Ltd.
Distribution Center	RK Building, 2nd Floor	130 Joo Seng Road
Airport Industrial Park	2-13-10 Shimo-Meguro,	#06-01/03
364 Innovation Drive	Meguro-Ku	Olivine Building
North Clarendon, VT 05759-9436	Tokyo 153 0064	Singapore 368357
Tel: (802) 773-8930	Tel: (03) 5437-0171	Tel: (65) 280-3320
Tel: (800) 526-2778	Fax: (03) 5437-0755	Fax: (65) 280-6290
Fax: (802) 773-6993		

Set in Giovanni Book on QuarkXPress
Printed in Singapore

First Edition
07 06 05 04 03 02   10 9 8 7 6 5 4 3 2 1